SACRED
GEOMETRY

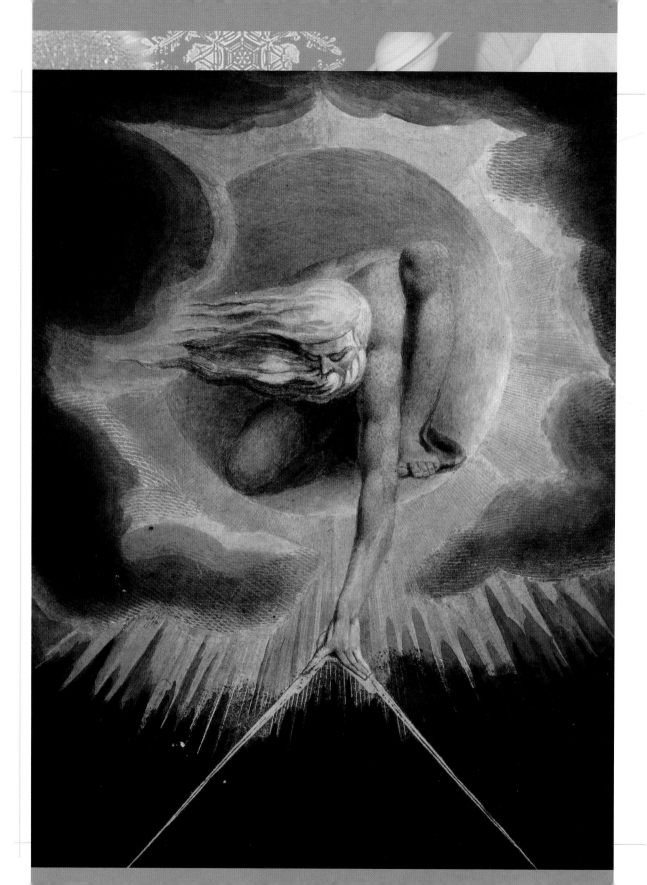

SACRED GEOMETRY

Deciphering the Code

Stephen Skinner

Sterling Publishing Co., Inc.
New York

Library of Congress Cataloging-in-Publication Data Available

10 9 8 7 6 5 4 3 2

Published in 2006 by Sterling Publishing Co., Inc.
387 Park Avenue South, New York, NY 10016

First published in the UK by Gaia Books
A division of Octopus Publishing Group Ltd

Copyright © 2006 by Octopus Publishing Group Ltd
Text copyright © 2006 Stephen Skinner

Distributed in Canada by Sterling Publishing
$^{c}/o$ Canadian Manda Group, 165 Dufferin Street,
Toronto, Canada M6K 3H6

Printed in China
All rights reserved

Sterling ISBN-13: 978-1-4027-4129-6
        ISBN-10: 1-4027-4129-4

For information about custom editions, special sales,
premium and corporate purchases, please contact
Sterling Special Sales Department at 800-805-5489
or specialsales@sterlingpub.com.

Contents

Introduction   6

PART 1   **THE HIDDEN ORDER**   14

CHAPTER 1   Pure arithmetic   16

CHAPTER 2   Pure geometry   40

PART 2   **THE GEOMETRY OF NATURE**   60

CHAPTER 3   Life's geometry   62

CHAPTER 4   Geometry in astronomy and cosmology   74

PART 3   **THE GEOMETRY OF THE MANMADE WORLD**   88

CHAPTER 5   Sacred geometry and the landscape   90

CHAPTER 6   Sacred geometry in architecture   116

CHAPTER 7   Sacred geometry in art   140

Conclusion   152

Bibliography   153

Index   156

Acknowledgements   160

Introduction

Geometry is a Greek word that literally means the 'measurement of the earth.' Long before it was committed to paper, geometry was concerned with the measurement of the land, a practice we today call surveying. Subsumed under geometry is the measurement and construction of buildings and the determination of the boundaries between one man's land and another's. At a more exalted level, geometry distinguishes between the domain of the sacred and the profane.

Euclid (325–265 BC) was the first to summarize in detail the axioms and theorems of this fascinating subject. What Euclid wrote in *Elements* on plane geometry is still completely valid and has not been superseded even after 2,000 years. What other type of geometry, perhaps more secret or sacred, might have survived hidden in the form of buildings or in the handiwork of nature?

Of course, not all geometry is sacred. Geometry was seen as being useful to site and construct buildings beneficial to those who inhabited them. When it was pleasing to the gods, it became 'sacred.' A temple, for example, may be hallowed if it is constructed according to certain sacred proportions and orientated in a specific direction. Such concerns with proportion and direction are so universal across so many cultures that they must reflect a reality. In this book I propose to search for those specific measurements that are sacred exactly because they help to hallow or make sacred such buildings: from Iron Age megalithic rings, through ancient Greek and Egyptian temples and Renaissance cathedrals to the very latest modern organic constructions.

Why geometry is sacred

Just as numbers were sacred for the Pythagoreans, so geometry was sacred for all ancient Greeks because it was the most concrete and yet the most abstract form of reasoning. Geometry, as we will see, is the archetypal patterning of many things, perhaps even all things, be they noumenal (something whose experience may be felt but not proved), conceptual, mathematical, natural or architectural.

Almost all ancient peoples created their temples and other sacred spaces with careful reference to the correct numbers, geometry and proportion. Geometry governed the very movement of the heavenly bodies and the seasons. The megalithic builders of Britain and the designers of the pyramids in Egypt applied this sacred geometry to the positioning and orientation of their constructions.

Geometry in its purest, simplest form is sacred. Yet it is founded on ordinary geometry and the geometric figures of Euclid—circles, triangles, squares—as well as ratios and harmonics. Just as growth is expressed by repeating patterns, so art and virtuosity in architecture are often expressed by harmony. What is harmony

but the (maybe subliminal) repetition of the same proportions. The parts of the whole do not even have to be in precisely the same proportion but can be an harmonic of that proportion.

The proportions that are sacred are governed by certain numbers, such as *phi,* Φ, (also called the Golden Mean). They occur again and again in the work of the ancient Greeks as well as the Gothic architects of the Middle Ages, and also in the growth of living things. Through these numbers the sacred geometry of living things and the perspectives of art and architecture coincide.

The study of sacred geometry

The ancient Greeks were the first civilization to establish the study of sacred numbers and geometry, although they

ABOVE The standing stones of Callanish on the Isle of Lewis, Scotland, from 1800 BC, were among the first stones to be surveyed by Alexander Thom.

BELOW The growth pattern of a logarithmic spiral maintains the same bearing/angle from its centre, no matter how large it grows.

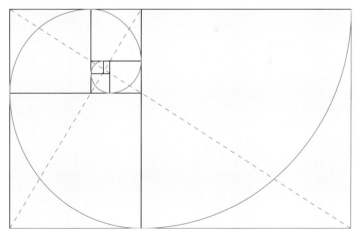

probably learned the basics from ancient Egypt. This knowledge was preserved by the Arab world during the early Middle Ages, and then started to return to western Europe in the 12th century with the appearance of translations of Arabic and Greek texts into Latin.

In the Middle Ages the basic university curriculum was called the *trivium*, which focused on grammar, rhetoric and logic. The more advanced course, however, was called the *quadrivium* (literally 'four subjects') and reflected the importance of geometry. It consisted of geometry, arithmetic, astronomy and music. These are all connected by the geometry of Euclid and the numbers of Pythagoras (sixth century BC). Music was seen as a matter of arithmetic—the precise arithmetic divisions between adjacent musical notes defined harmony and so formed an arithmetic you could hear. Astronomy relied on arithmetic to calculate the movements of the heavenly

bodies, while geometry defined the relationships between all three. I propose to examine some of the secrets of the *quadrivium*, which is no longer taught and to a large extent no longer appreciated.

Of course, the study of sacred geometry has attracted some pretty strange theories and theorists, particularly in the last 30 years. As the internationally renowned astrophysicist Dr Mario Livio wrote in his book *The Golden Ratio*, it is possible to draw all sorts of geometric figures over any site plan, but if the major vertices of these do not fall on an actual physical point, intersection or corner, the conclusions drawn from such a figure are at best arbitrary and at worst nonsense.

The need for whole numbers

Egyptian and ancient Greek civilizations used the circle, ellipse, triangle, square, and rectangle to derive harmonious proportions for their tombs and temples. Their geometers were interested in Pythagorean right-angled triangles (for a variety of reasons), the associated square roots, the relationship of a circle to a square, exact whole number ratios of sacred numbers such as 9 (particularly unitary fractions that have 1 as the numerator), and the relationships between the volumes of different buildings.

At all times, from the pyramids of ancient Egypt to the Gothic cathedrals of the Middle Ages, the emphasis was on *whole* number dimensions that were easily measurable. To a much lesser extent, they used irrational ratios such as the Golden Section (known by the Greek letter *phi*, Φ, and the same as the Golden Mean), which generates the logarithmic spiral, one of the basic curves of life and growth.

BELOW The Pythagorean *lambda*, showing the connection between even numbers and the intervals of the muscial scale, constructing a harmonic system.

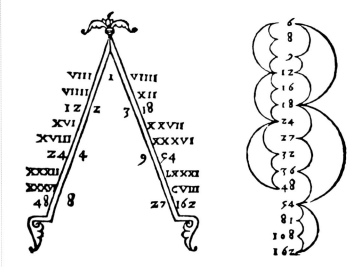

Pythagoras showed how whole numbers are basic to creation because of the way they define harmony, both in music and the heavenly spheres. We had to wait for Johannes Kepler (1571–1630) to discover the exact ratios between the period and diameter of planetary orbits to see this confirmed. The architect Sir Christopher Wren helped to prove the astronomical ratios, and he embodied sacred geometry into St Paul's Cathedral in London.

Repeating patterns and forms

Plato (427–347 BC) believed that all things grew from forms, simple 3-D geometry and immutable patterns that shape the backbone of reality. For too long his ideas were considered mystical, but the physical importance of simple forms and numbers is now being confirmed by physicists and biologists who have discovered essentially simple formulae, such as the structure of DNA (based on the geometry of the helix and the pentagon) and the pattern of leaf growth in plants (based on a fixed geometric angle).

The Roman architect Vitruvius (first century BC) articulated mathematical proportion and harmony in building construction. When the details of his work were rediscovered in Europe they set the stage for the buildings of the Renaissance created by the likes of Leonardo da Vinci (1452–1519) and Donato Bramante (1444–1514), who were as much artists and geometricians as architects.

Sacred geometry was also very much alive in the Islamic world where the representation of human and animal forms was forbidden. Tile patterns, tessellations and timeless architectural features—the cupola, half-dome, tunnel

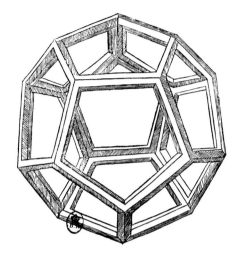

LEFT Leonardo da Vinci's illustration of a regular icosahedron, from Luca Pacioli's book *De divina proportione*.

vault, horseshoe arch and pendant stalactite forms—became the concrete mode of geometric expression.

Gothic architecture absorbed elements of both Greek geometry and Vitruvian proportion. Master masons injected geometric and numerical symbolism into their buildings. Unexpectedly, the circle, rather than the triangle or the square as is often asserted, became the basic controlling device for Gothic cathedral design. Numerical symbolism was rife, and circles, rectangles and other polygons were generated with harmonious and 'heavenly' proportions.

With the Renaissance came a renewed and voracious interest in Classical theories. Aristotle's works formed the basis of the most heated debates, as theologians attempted to reconcile his experimental approach to the world with the received and fixed cosmological doctrines of Ptolemy. Strangely, it was not Christian doctrine versus Greek philosophy, but Greek (Ptolemy championed by the

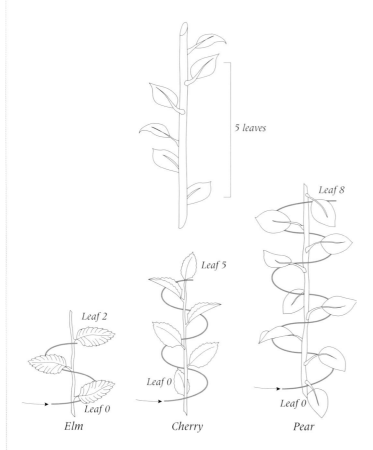

5 leaves

Leaf 8

Leaf 5

Leaf 2

Leaf 0

Leaf 0

Leaf 0

Elm

Cherry

Pear

ABOVE **Counting leaf growth on the stems of the elm, cherry and pear, each yielding a Fibonacci number. The angles between leaves can be determined by dividing the number of turns (each turn 360 degrees) by the number of leaves sprouted over the distance.**

Alberti (1404–1472) remarked that a building must appear whole like an organism. Practical as always, Leonardo made his famous drawing of Vitruvius' *homo quadratus* to see if the cubit was a valid measure.

Repeating patterns and forms in nature, such as the helix and logarithmic spiral, the geometry of plant growth and the fractal, are products of the internal geometry of growth. Leonardo loved to observe and draw living structures, anatomy, birds' wings, trees, waves, and water flow. His namesake, Leonardo of Pisa (*c*.1170–*c*.1240) had discovered a series of numbers that would become known as the Fibonacci series—its application in charting the repeating patterns of natural growth took a long time to materialize.

Organic forms inspired architecture, such as Antonio Gaudí's cathedral in Barcelona, as well as artistic styles such as art nouveau and surrealism. They culminated in the complex geometry of structures, such as the Goetheanum in Switzerland and the Sydney Opera House, where culture has to an extent replaced religion as the patron of sacred geometry.

A bridge between the gods and man
The purpose of a temple, church or mosque is to provide a sacred space for people to communicate with and worship their gods. By being sacred the space is closer to god, facilitates prayer and is a locus for priests. The space is truly sacred when it is sufficiently pure and correct in its structure for the god to indwell.

The prime conditions of a sacred space have always been a suitably proportioned architecture, situated on the right spot and

Christian Church) against Greek (Aristotle championed by the Humanists). Hermetic texts and Greek and Arabic translations of more practical works leavened the intellectual ferment.

Thinkers such as Leonardo viewed art, architecture and anatomy in the same light, utilizing one in pursuit of the others. Architectural harmony and proportion could be based on human form or the projective geometry of perspective. Michelangelo (1475–1564) said that knowledge of the human figure was vital to a comprehension of architecture. Leon

facing in the right direction. Let us look at these in reverse order.

The direction faced has always been a key issue: mosques face Mecca, while Hindu temples (mostly) and Christian cathedrals (on the whole) face east. There are notable exceptions, such as Chartres Cathedral in France, which faces northeast. Megalithic monuments, such as Stonehenge in England (which also faces northeast), have distinct orientations: they are orientated to other nearby monuments via ley lines and often incorporate astro-nomical alignments related to the Sun and the Moon. Sacred geometry is needed to locate and align such sacred structures.

In the past it was of the greatest importance to site churches, temples and megalithic standing stones on a 'location of power'. In imperial China (and increasingly again in our own times) the practice of *feng shui* has been used to find the *hsueh*, or dragon point, to provide maximum energy to important buildings, especially palaces, temples and tombs.

ABOVE The swirling patterns of a daisy flower seedhead utilize the geometry of the Golden Spiral, which is based on the Fibonacci series.

The early Christian Church went as far as to issue directives that, in every case possible, new churches should be sited on old pagan 'power spots'. This, of course, was considered desirable for three reasons: the priestly geometricians of the church would harness the power, worshippers of the old religion would continue to come to the site, and the original pagan artefacts would be destroyed. This has interesting impli-cations when we come to look at the geometry of ley lines.

Lastly, but most importantly, the structure itself must adhere to certain geometric rules. Such rules have been well documented—for example, the exact

ABOVE The spires of Chartres Cathedral, symbolizing the Sun and the Moon, are the most obvious of much geometric symbolism embedded in its design.

RIGHT The structure of unfurling ferns follows a repetitive pattern.

BELOW The mysterious tor at Glastonbury is a focal point for surrounding ley alignments and New Age pilgrims alike.

dimensions of King Solomon's original Temple in Jerusalem were recorded in at least two places in the Bible, and the subsequent rebuilding (twice) of this Temple has occasioned further discussion of the sacred geometry of the building. In fact, in Victorian times people, such as Sir William Stirling, wrote whole volumes about the sacred dimensions of the Temple. The architecture of Gothic cathedrals were, in turn, based on these recorded dimensions.

The Greeks, as the inventors of the main body of geometry, applied it in detail when they constructed their temples. Greek architecture was not always based on the vaunted Golden Section but, as is the case with the Parthenon, based on unitary fractions and volumes. In Egypt the sacred geometry of the Great Pyramid is dependent more upon *seked* measure (see page 117) than the Golden Mean, although the latter does occur. Rather surprisingly, the sacred geometry of the Hebrews, Greeks and Egyptians ratios has measuring units in common.

Of course, sacred geometry is also sacred because it is often the pattern behind God's handiwork—from the structure of crystals and the water flow in a river to the way a palm frond unfurls or an ammonite grows its shell—or just simply in the process of growth itself.

The tradition lives on

In the last several hundred years many attempts have been made to retro-fit sacred geometry to the Great Pyramid in Egypt, including totally contorted interpretations of the Bible based on pyramid dimensions measured in fractions of an inch. Only in the late 20th century

was it realized that the dimensions expressed in whole royal cubits conform to simple Euclidean geometry. Likewise the careful study and measurement of European megalithic structures—dating back easily as far as the pyramids of ancient Egypt—and the ley lines connecting them also relied upon a very distinct sacred geometry measured in whole numbers of megalithic yards.

The message that comes through loud and clear is that ancient man was every bit as clever as modern man. The geometry he used in his buildings (which have lasted thousands of years, rather longer than the average life of 100 years for a modern structure) is still not fully appreciated, understood or utilized by modern man. This geometry, which Euclid enunciated so many millennia ago, is only now being seen as part of the forms behind the fabric of life and as an integral part of the constructional method of the Great Geometer.

ABOVE **The Parthenon, built to embody the most subtle geometry of the ancient Greeks, has stood for more than two thousands years.**

LEFT **The forms of nature, such as the spectacular organic curves of the Sydney Opera House, now form the basis of many secular buildings.**

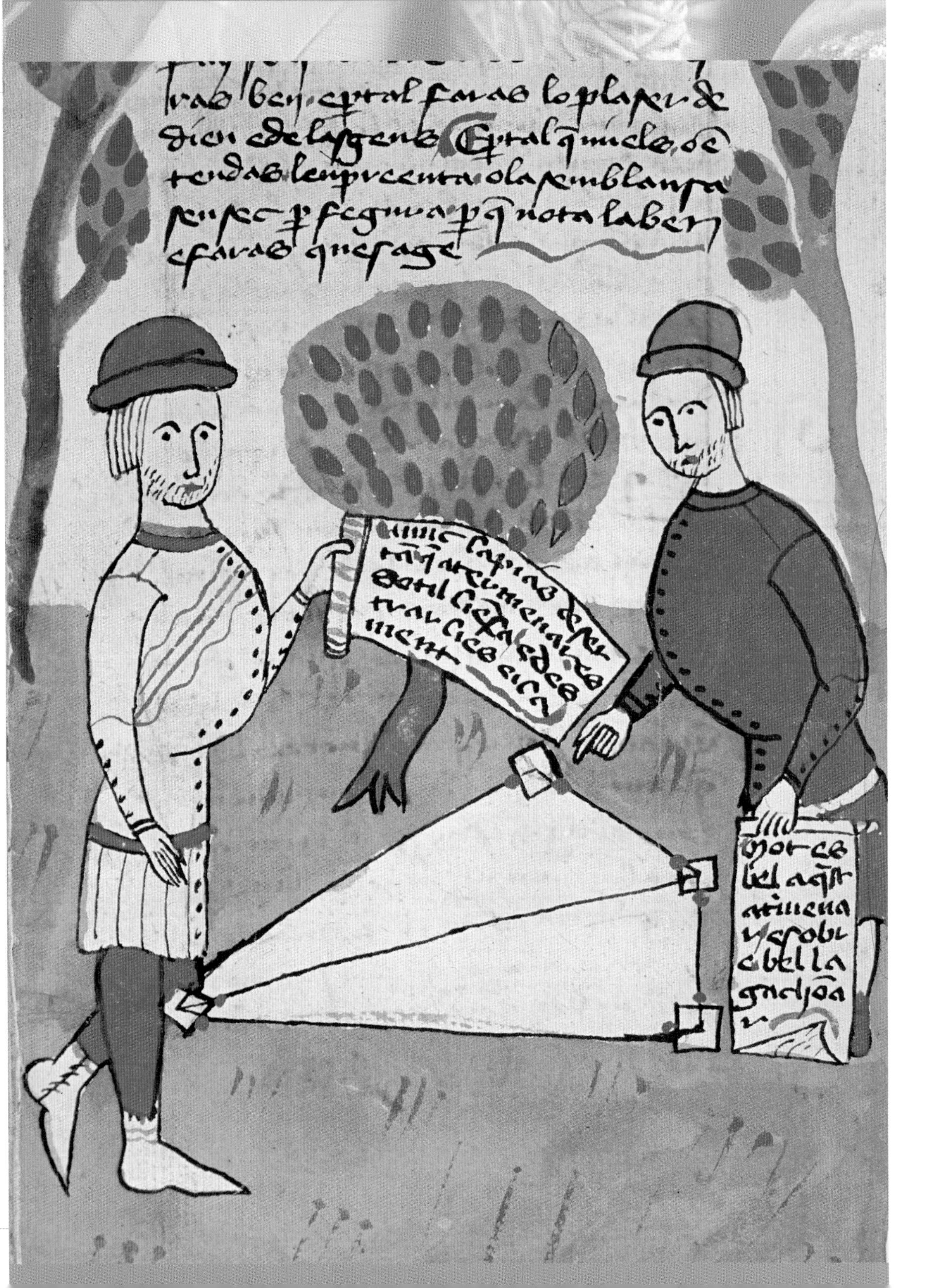

PART 1

THE HIDDEN ORDER

The Greeks were the first to codify geometry. For them it was a pure abstract science akin to logic, based on underlying truths, unlike the practical science favoured by the Egyptians. Geometry provided the Greeks with an absolute truth that could be proved over and over again with the simplest of tools—a compass and a straight-edged ruler.

The Greeks conceived the creator of the universe in terms of absolute truth, not in terms of handed-down dogma, received wisdom or religious belief. They deduced that form and number were essential to the universe and that creation proceeded from abstract forms—things that could be intellectually appreciated, but not grasped or perceived by the five senses—to physical reality. The subtleties of number and the absoluteness of geometry were part of the noumenal world, the hidden structure behind physical matter.

Geometry and numbers are sacred because they codify the hidden order behind creation. They are the instruments used to create the physical universe. Simplicity in number, fraction and ratio provide the harmony and intellectual rigor of both the universe and the geometry of Euclid and his fellow Greek geometers. The concrete application of the universality of these numbers—and the proof—embodied in music and measurement.

LEFT **Thirteenth-century surveyors measuring the land using right-angled triangles and triangulation methods.**

CHAPTER 1
PURE ARITHMETIC

Pythagoras takes pride of place as the first major philosopher to state clearly that numbers in themselves are sacred and exist in their own right. He made distinctions between various types of number, separating the prime numbers and the perfect numbers from the rest. His division of numbers into odd and even created the *lambda*, λ, a figure whose properties still stimulate modern mathematicians and physicists to discover new things about the periodic table of elements and the universe.

Pythagoras' discovery that whole numbers governed musical harmonies convinced him that harmony and planning lay behind the complex universe. He reasoned that if whole numbers created harmonious sounds, as distinct from discordant ones, numbers must be behind the harmony of the universe at every level, from the paths of the planets to the strings of a lyre.

For archaeologists to determine the important numbers that helped to create the measurements of a particular building, they have to know what special units the original architects used. Finally, we look at *phi*, a most intriguing number and one that generates the self-replicating Golden Mean, which is found again and again, both in nature and in the sacred geometry of many buildings.

Pythagoras and the worship of number

Pythagoras declared that numbers themselves were sacred—they had a separate and real existence and were not just convenient counting markers. The regularities derived from such numbers, be they musical, astronomical or architectural, were also sacred. This idea is at the root of sacred geometry. In fact, Pythagoras could be called the 'father of sacred geometry.'

Pythagoras (569– c.475 BC) was born on the island of Samos in the Aegean Sea. He also lived in the Greek colony of Croton in southern Italy and spent as many as 20 years in Egypt where he learned both mathematics and philosophy. He may even have been to Babylon, where he would have encountered Babylonian mathematics.

Pythagoras is undoubtedly the foremost among those who investigated the sacred and mystical properties of numbers, but he also strayed into geometry. He probably learned the theorem named after him in Egypt or Babylon. Pythagoras' Theorem defined the lengths of the sides of any right-angled triangle (see pages 44–45). He proved that the length of the side (hypotenuse) opposite the right (90-degree) angle was, if squared, equal to the sum of the squares of the other two sides.

Draw a right-angled triangle with the two shorter sides (*a* and *b*) measuring exactly one unit and two units long respectively. You can then determine the length of the hypotenuse using Pythagoras' Theorem:

The length of the hypotenuse^2
= side a^2 + side b^2

To find the length of the hypotenuse, square the length of both of the short sides and add them together:

Hypotenuse^2 = 1^2 + 2^2 = 1 + 4 = 5

Therefore, the hypotenuse
= square root of 5 (or √5 or 2.2360679)

Thus, arithmetic and geometry are inextricably linked. If you measure the sides of a number of right-angled triangles you will soon find that there is a range of typical whole-number dimensions that fit this theorem and that are therefore called Pythagorean Triplets.

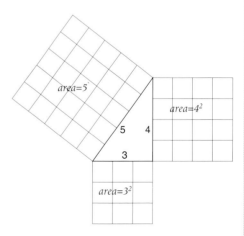

ABOVE **A Pythagorean triangle proving that the sum of the squares on two sides equals the square on the hypotenuse. This is shown graphically here as 3^2 + 4^2 = 5^2.**

PYTHAGOREAN TRIPLETS

Side a	Side b	Hypotenuse
3	4	5
7	24	25
8	15	17
17	144	145

Pythagorean Triplets were seen as significant magical numbers. They can be found listed on Babylonian tablets dating as far back as 1600 BC.

In his quest to understand the nature of harmony, and hence the machinery of the universe, Pythagoras investigated allied fields such as music and discovered the arithmetic behind musical intervals and the pitch of notes (see pages 22–23).

Pythagoras reasoned that if numbers can perfectly represent the harmonies of music, they could also represent the harmonies of the cosmos itself. Further confirmation came from the mathematical (although complex) regularity of the movements of the planets and other heavenly bodies (although Pythagoras did not actually compute these orbits as ellipses). Pythagoras also equated the notes of the nine Greek Muses with the movements and sounds of the nine heavenly bodies (the seven planets, the sphere of the fixed stars and a strange concept called counter-Earth).

The holy *tetractys*

An example of the way in which the regularities of numbers become sacred can be found in the *tetractys*, in which the Pythagoreans displayed the first four numbers (1, 2, 3, 4) in a triangular form.

Triangles are the most stable of geometric figures. The base of this triangle consists of the number 4 (the number of justice and order as far as the Pythagoreans were concerned). This figure was referred to as the holy *tetractys* and reputedly contained the password by which Pythagoreans recognized one another.

Adding up all the numbers in each line of the *tetractys* (1 + 2 + 3 + 4) generates

```
         X
       X   X
     X   X   X
   X   X   X   X
```

ABOVE **The holy *tetractys*, a Pythagorean figure showing that numbers 1 to 4 add up to 10, or the decad, the symbol of completion.**

the decad (10), which was considered to be the completion of a full cycle. Indeed, it is in the decimal system, the Kabbalah, the Heavenly Stems of the Chinese and in a number of other traditions.

Lambda and the harmony of the world

The twelfth letter of the Greek alphabet is *lambda*, λ, which is a bit like an upside down V. The Pythagoreans inscribed seven numbers (1, 2, 3, 4, 8, 9 and 27) in the shape of *lambda* (see page 19). This Pythagorean *lambda* symbolizes many things, such as:

• Even numbers (with the exception of 1, which might more properly be on the apex itself) are arrayed down the left side of the *lambda*. These are referred to as female numbers, as they include duality and therefore have the potential to split and reproduce. The female has tradition-ally been associated with the left side in most cultures.

• Odd numbers down the right side are male. The ancient Chinese also held the same view that creation began with the number one (which for them was male), which split into two (yin and yang) and progressed with an even balance of the sexes. The male has traditionally been associated with the right side.

• The numbers of the left side consist of multiples of 2—or, as we might say it in the computer age, the binary arithmetic of the powers of 2.

• The left hand of the *lambda* consists of powers of 3.

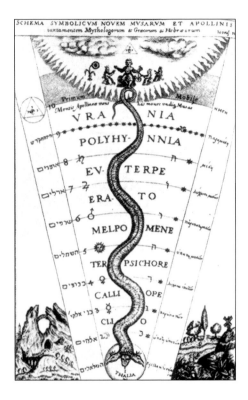

ABOVE The Nine Spheres descending from Heaven to Earth, with the Nine Muses from Thalia (Earth) through Clio (Moon) to Urania (Apollo enthroned) above the fixed stars.

sitting at their desks. The figure on the right is Pythagoras (look closely at his banner) using pebbles to calculate. The figure on the left is Boethius using the new Arabic/Hindu numerals to calculate. The *lambda* appears in the middle of the female figure's skirt, unifying both styles of arithmetic.

During the Renaissance, many thinkers attempted to synthesize the elements of Classical Greek culture, which arrived in Europe at the end of the first millennium via translations of Greek works into Arabic. The Greek originals had been swept away by the tide of barbarism and Christian zeal that spread over Europe after the collapse of the Roman Empire. In the illustration below you can see how the *lambda* is correlated with intervals of the musical scale in the engraving from Francesco Giorgi's (1466–1540) book *De harmonia mundi* (Of the Harmony of the World) published in 1525, which ties together the *lambda*, Pythagoras' numbers and the musical scale.

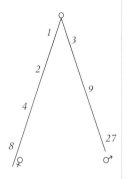

ABOVE The *lambda* represents the Pythagorean division of the numbers into odd or masculine (right) and even or feminine (left).

BELOW A version of the *lambda* compared with the musical scale, by Francesco Giorgi, a Franciscan friar of Venice. Note that the Z should be read as 2.

• Plato, in his *Timaeus*, used the *lambda* to explain musical scales (see pages 22–23).

Lambda in the Renaissance

The *lambda* was of great importance in the Renaissance. The illustration on page 20, dating from 1525, shows the different types of arithmetic. The central female figure is meant to be Arithmetic herself. Around her head (in a Renaissance cartoon style) is the banner *Typus arithmeticae*, in other words the types of arithmetic symbolized by the two men

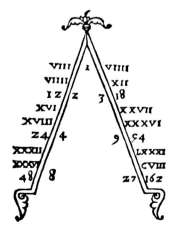

The surprising secrets of the *lambda*

Anyone who looks at the *lambda* will eventually ask, why did Pythagoras stop at just seven numbers? Was it because seven was a magical number? Perhaps he, like the clever teacher he was, wanted us to ask what comes next, although it is fairly obvious that the answer on each leg is 16 and 81.

ABOVE **Arithmetic in a red dress (with *lambda*) points to Pythagoras (her left), counting with pebbles, and Boethius with new style Arabic numbers (her right).**

Sweet sixteen

The number 16—the next number on the left side of the *lambda*—figures in the hexadecimal system that runs computers (now doubled and redoubled to 64 to give faster 64-bit computing). The number 16 has also formed the basis of the second-most popular system of divination in Europe during the Renaissance and later. I refer, of course, to the system of geomancy, the 16 geomantic figures from *via* to *laetitia*, which was second only to astrology in importance in Europe. It disappeared until its resurrection by the Hermetic Order of the Golden Dawn at the end of the 19th century.

Geomancy is, strictly speaking, a system of divination by dots or sand marking, resulting in 16 binary figures. It has absolutely nothing to do with the Chinese practice of *feng shui*. Despite this, around 1870 the Reverend Yates, an English missionary, struggling to find an equivalent word for the Chinese characters *feng shui*, seized upon 'geomancy' because his dictionary happened vaguely to mention 'earth' and 'divination'. He did not pause to think that the word actually referred to a completely unrelated and already existing European practice. As a result, the word stuck as a translation of *feng shui*.

Many of the investigators of ley lines and other Iron Age geometrical landscape features (see pages 102–105) started to draw parallels with *feng shui* and, unfortunately, began to refer to their own ley-line research as 'geomancy.'

Eighty-one

The next number on the right side of the *lambda* is 81 or 3^4 or 9 x 9. This is a number that receives scant respect from numerologists but is very significant in terms of the structure of the universe. Its importance is foreshadowed by IAO, the Gnostic name of God, whose letters add together to 81. This value is calculated with the system of Greek *isopsephy* (or to use the Kabbalistic term, *gematria*), which was common even before Pythagoras' time by assigning numbers to letters:

I (10) + A (1) + O (omicron) (70) = 81
I (10) + A (1) + O (omega) (800) = 811

The modern-day *lambda*

The modern Pythagorean Dr. Peter Plichta has rediscovered several of the secrets of the *lambda* and applied them to modern chemistry. Dr. Plichta is a polymath with degrees in chemistry and physics, yet he thinks like a Pythagorean and accepts that numbers are real and separately existing parts of the framework behind the physical universe.

Dr. Plichta is fascinated by prime numbers. Why, for example, do they appear randomly in the number series as we count from 1 onward and not in some regular order? In fact, they get rarer as we progress. He recalled Hadamard's Prime Number Law (1896), which indicated that the decrease in the frequency of prime numbers popping up in the number sequence from 1 to infinity was related to Euler's number, the natural logarithm $e = 2.718$. He realized that this number also governed various natural laws, such as radioactive disintegration and escape velocity, and wondered if the prime numbers also governed nature in a similar way.

He first thought of the periodic table of the elements, which is fascinating for

anyone interested in the order of the universe. The stable elements are made up of elements with atomic numbers 1, 2, 3 ... 83. Beyond 83 (bismuth), elements such as 90 (thorium) or 92 (uranium) are unstable. Indeed, some are created only under laboratory conditions and later break down into other elements, specifically 91, 89, 88, 87, 86, 85, and 84.

Now, for some strange reason the elements with atomic numbers 43 and 61 (technetium and promethium) do not exist naturally, even elsewhere in the solar system. So, in fact, there are exactly 81 stable elements, the number of IAO and the key *lambda* number. Another strange Pythagorean fact is that elements can have up to 10 variant forms (or isotopes) but *never* any more. As Pythagoras had declared, 10 is the number of completion.

1 H																	2 He
3 Li	4 Be											5 B	6 C	7 N	8 O	9 F	10 Ne
11 Na	12 Mg											13 Al	14 Si	15 P	16 S	17 Cl	18 Ar
19 K	20 Ca	21 Sc	22 Ti	23 V	24 Cr	25 Mn	26 Fe	27 Co	28 Ni	29 Cu	30 Zn	31 Ga	32 Ge	33 As	34 Se	35 Br	36 Kr
37 Rb	38 Sr	39 Y	40 Zr	41 Nb	42 Mo	43 Tc	44 Ru	45 Rh	46 Pd	47 Ag	48 Cd	49 In	50 Sn	51 Sb	52 Te	53 I	54 Xe
55 Cs	56 Ba	57 *La	72 Hf	73 Ta	74 W	75 Re	76 Os	77 Ir	78 Pt	79 Au	80 Hg	81 Tl	82 Pb	83 Bi	84 Po	85 At	86 Rn
87 Fr	88 Ra	89 +Ac	104 Rf	105 Ha	106 Sg	107 Ns	108 Hs	109 Mt	110 Ds	111 Rg	112 Uub	113 Uug					

58 Ce	59 Pr	60 Nd	61 Pm	62 Sm	63 Eu	64 Gd	65 Tb	66 Dy	67 Ho	68 Er	69 Tm	70 Yb	71 Lu
90 H	91 Pa	92 U	93 Np	94 Pu	95 Am	96 Cm	97 Bk	98 Cf	99 Es	100 Fm	101 Md	102 No	103 Lr

ABOVE **The periodic table of the elements shows just 81 stable elements. The elements shown in yellow are either unstable or do not occur in nature.**

Music, vibration and whole numbers

We hear sound, and therefore music, by sensing vibrations in air. Pitch (how high or low a sound is) reflects the vibration's 'speed' or frequency. Stringed instruments allow more than one note to be played at a time, and notes that are played simultaneously on an instrument can sound harmonious or discordant. Surprisingly, this is not dependent on your musical preferences but on an objective, arithmetic order that underlies vibrating strings and all music.

Play a note by plucking a string on a guitar, then halve the length of the string by pressing it on the fingerboard with a finger and pluck it again. You hear a higher note—double the frequency of the first one. It is actually the same note but an octave above ('octave' refers to the eight notes of a major scale, see right). Stopping (or shortening) the string at other points along the fingerboard creates different notes, which are other fractional lengths, or ratios, of the original note.

BELOW Robert Fludd's vision of the monochord dividing up the universe and the musical scale with the same arithmetical divisions.

Harmonious ratios

What is remarkable is that only whole number ratios produce harmonious results—the ratio of the vibrational frequency of the musical octave is 2:1. If the ratios of the strings were altered to, say, 4.2 or 3.7 units in length, the result would be dissonant. This discovery confirmed Pythagoras' belief that there is something special, even sacred, in whole numbers. In music these whole-number ratios form scales, the building blocks of music. Each ratio has a name, and the ones in

bold in the table below form a major diatonic scale (the *doh-re-mi* scale familiar to most of us), here in the key of C major. The ratios remain constant for any key.

The character of scales

There are many scales with different musical characters. A minor scale, which uses the minor third rather than the major

SCALE INTERVALS AND RATIOS

NAME	RATIO	NOTE	
Tonic (first or root note)	**1:1**	**C**	Unison—the same note
Second	**8:9**	**D**	
Minor Third	5:6	E flat	
Major Third	**4:5**	**E**	
Fourth	**3:4**	**F**	
Fifth	**2:3**	**G**	
Minor Sixth	5:8	A flat	
Major Sixth	**3:5**	**A**	
Minor Seventh	9:16	B flat	Called the dominant seventh
Major Seventh	**8:15**	**B**	
Octave (8 notes above)	**1:2**	**C**	The note one octave higher, double the frequency
Twelfth	1:3	G	A fifth over the octave

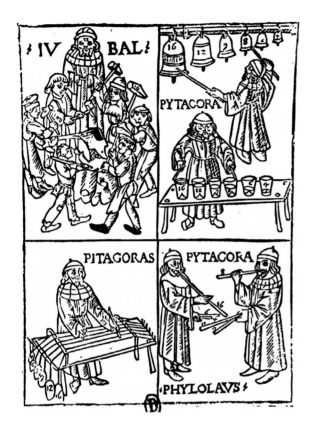

LEFT Pythagoras discovers the arithmetical harmony of sound. Note that the hammers, bells, glasses, strings, and flutes are all calibrated 4, 6, 8, 9, 12, and 16.

English hymns as well as folk and popular music—'Amazing Grace', for example, has a major pentatonic melody.

Adding a note between the fourth and fifth of a minor pentatonic scale—the famous 'blue note' in blues, jazz and rock music—also has a very powerful character. Non-European cultures have different musical scales—for example, the Chinese use pentatonic scales and Indians 22 notes, as in one Persian scale—but the principle of whole number ratios always holds good.

The beauty of harmony

Now here comes the clincher. If you draw the bow of a violin over a tuned metal plate sprinkled with light powder (lycopodium powder is best), the grains line up in complex patterns. So not only do sacred numbers govern planetary orbits and musical harmony, but these notes also create beautiful geometric forms. It shows the direct relevance of certain numbers to certain patterns of notes and hence to certain geometrical patterns, and these patterns are beautiful. Likewise architecture, as in the Parthenon, drawn from sacred numbers and their combinations, has a beauty that we can feel instinctively, but may not have realized is based firmly on the underlying sacred arithmetic and geometry.

third, is often regarded as melancholic. The change (known as a cadence) from a major chord to its minor version is particularly haunting. The reverse, from minor to major, known as a Picardy third, is regarded as uplifting or hopeful.

Musicians use the character of different scales and cadences to demonstrate the profound emotional potential deriving from Pythagoras' underlying arithmetic. For him, musical harmony was further confirmation that whole numbers and unitary fractions are sacred while inexact fractions are not. Pentatonic (five-note) scales—the major version has the same ratios as the black notes on the piano— occur in folk music worldwide and are familiar to all of us. They appear in

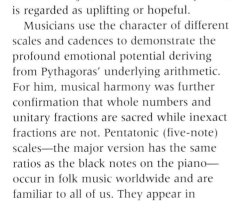

BELOW A pattern produced by sprinkling powder on a plate and drawing a violin bow across it to produce a particular frequency.

The value of fractions

In the past people used to count in 12s or 60s and divide these numbers by 2, 3, 4 or another number in their head. It was easier to work with 12 or 60 because they can be divided evenly by many other numbers. Ten cannot be so divided. The whole essence of counting boils down to calculating fractions of a whole and the proportions of its parts.

Ten is divisible only by 2 and 5 and so is not very flexible. Twelve, however, is divisible by 2, 3, 4, and 6. Sixty is much better as it can be subdivided by 2, 3, 4, 5, 6, 10, 12, 15, 20, and 30. You get the idea. So instead of the absolutely infinite range of decimals you can instead break things down quite finely using a much smaller set of fractions, such as 1/60, 2/60, 3/60 and so on.

A hundred years ago it would be natural to think of seven eggs in a box holding a dozen eggs as 7/12 of the contents of the box. Modern mathematics demands a decimal answer of 0.5833333. No ancient civilization would have dreamed of using 0.5833333 for such a simple thing—they would have used simple fractions. Many fractions or relationships can be neatly represented by one whole number divided by another such as 7/12 or 2/3 (rather than 0.6666666). Such a system can also express fractions as ratios. So 7/12 is the same as 7:12 and 2/3 is the same as 2:3. Fractions are more memorable, easier to deal with and more often the exact value that needs to be expressed.

Choosing the best divisor

The choice of the divisor (or denominator, the lower part of the fraction) is of great importance, so we need to discover what divisors were used by any particular group of architects, builders or civilization. Once we have established that, we can translate all of the modern precise measurements made in meters, yards, feet, and inches into the system used by the original builders. Once those whole numbers are available, then the picture becomes much clearer and we can set about examining the symbolism, the meaning and the use of the buildings.

Let's use a very simple and fictional example. If you found a building that measured 666 units in length (never mind what the units are for the moment) rather than 1,811.5367 feet (552.1563 m), then you might reasonably deduce that the building had something to do with

BELOW Twelve items can be accommodated more naturally in an almost square box, but 10 items do not pack nearly as conveniently.

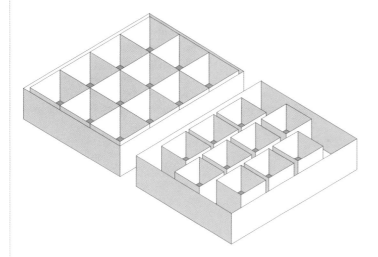

The Ninths

One significant set of decimals is expressed much more easily as ninths, which are particularly important in Greek measurements (¹⁰⁄₉ is the conversion factor between the standard Greek foot and the antique one):

0.111 ... = ⅑
0.222 ... = ²⁄₉
0.333 ... = ³⁄₉ = ⅓

And the pattern keeps repeating even beyond 1:

1.111 ... = ¹⁰⁄₉
1.222 ... = ¹¹⁄₉
1.333 ... = ¹²⁄₉

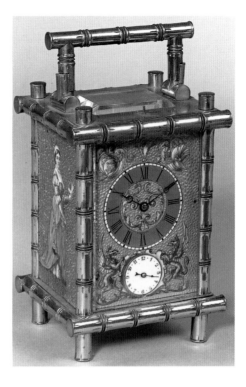

LEFT **French clockmakers successfully resisted the decimalization of time, and clocks still measure 60 minutes to the hour rather than 100.**

the Sun (666 is a solar symbolic number) or even with the Beast of Revelations. If it measured 1,811.5367 feet (552.1563 m) you would make no such deduction. I have used a symbolic number that most readers should recognize just to make the point. So in this book I will try to give both the modern measure and, where possible, the ancient unit figures as well. The logic of such measurements will enable us to say a lot more about the sacred geometry of the building.

When we are working out conversion factors between modern and ancient measures it soon becomes apparent that different peoples, places and civilizations of the ancient world shared the same specific units. It also becomes clear that there were definite connections between measures of apparently disparate things, such as length, weight, volume and even time. This unity seems to corroborate the presence of real and meaningful ancient measures.

ANCIENT AND MODERN MEASURES

Measures convert to	Metric(cm)	Metric(m)	Imperial(in)	Imperial (ft)
1 megalithic inch	2.074	0.020	0.816	0.068
1 megalithic yard	82.966	0.829	32.664	2.722
1 megalithic rod	497.799	4.977	195.984	16.332
1 standard cubit	44.893	0.448	17.674	1.472
1 royal cubit	52.375	0.523	20.620	1.718
1 remen	74.069	0.740	29.156	2.429
1 Roman foot	29.260	0.292	11.52	0.96
1 Greek foot	30.48	0.3048	12	1
1 Greek trimmed foot	33.866	0.338	13.333	1.111
1 Greek stadia	18288	182.88	7200	600
1 Greek plethron	3048	30.48	1200	100

Measuring the Earth with two sticks

Much of what modern science lays claim to was, in fact, discovered thousands of years ago, then lost during the Middle Ages. One of these facts is that the Earth is spherical, and the geometer concerned actually measured the circumference of the Earth to an incredible degree of accuracy ... using just two sticks.

ABOVE Eratosthenes, the man who measured the circumference of the world more than 22 centuries ago using just basic geometry and observation.

BELOW An obelisk at Alexandria whose shadow changed in length over the year. This might have suggested the method to Eratosthenes.

A new unit of measurement is often related to some naturally occurring phenomenon. The most obvious standards are the human body (cubit, palm, finger), astronomical (day, year) or the Earth (length of a degree of longitude). We cannot say with certainty what was used to create all the ancient standards of length, weight or time, but we know such measures were considered sacred.

When the French decided in the early 19th century to create the meter as their standard of length they based it upon one-40,000,000th of the circumference of the Earth. How were they going to measure this? They followed a method that was no more sophisticated than the method of

Eratosthenes (*c.*275–194 BC), a Greek geometer living in Egypt more than 2,000 years previously.

Shadow angles

Eratosthenes reasoned that, as the Earth was a sphere, he could use the Sun and the geometry of parallel lines to help measure the circumference of the Earth. He (or his assistants) travelled to the city of Syene (near modern-day Aswan in Egypt) and found the spot where, exactly at noon on the summer solstice (about 21st June in the Northern Hemisphere), the Sun would be directly overhead. This is the moment when the Sun reaches its most northerly point in the year (it is marked by the Tropic of Cancer on modern maps) and a vertical rod casts no shadow.

At exactly the same moment, he measured the angle of the shadow cast by a rod in Alexandria, the northernmost city in Egypt where he was head librarian of the great library. The angle was 7 degrees 12 minutes.

The Sun's rays at both Syene and Alexandria are parallel and so, by using simple Euclidian geometry (as shown in the diagram), he deduced that the angle made by the position of these two cities with the center of the Earth is also 7 degrees 12 minutes. Alexandria was 5,000 *stadia* from Syene, so he reasoned that:

If 7 degrees 12 minutes (i.e. 7.2 degrees)
= 5000 *stadia*, then 360 degrees (the Earth's circumference)
= 5000 x 360 / 7.2 = 250,000 *stadia*

250,000 *stadia* is 24,461 miles (39,186 km), which is a remarkably accurate measurement to have calculated for a man with two sticks and a measuring wheel in two cities in ancient Egypt. The modern mean estimate (using all sorts of expensive technology) of the circumference of the Earth is 24,891 miles (39,875 km), just 1.7 per cent different!

This is an experiment that any of us could in theory do today, but its essence lies in accurate measurement and a knowledge of basic geometry. The French measurement, incidentally, was slightly wrong as they did not take into account the slight flattening of the Earth at the North and South Poles.

ABOVE A rare colonial brass theodolite calibrated in degrees.

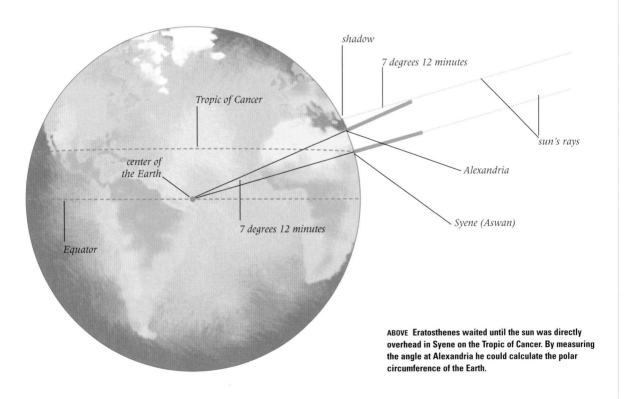

shadow

7 degrees 12 minutes

sun's rays

Tropic of Cancer

center of the Earth

Alexandria

7 degrees 12 minutes

Syene (Aswan)

Equator

ABOVE Eratosthenes waited until the sun was directly overhead in Syene on the Tropic of Cancer. By measuring the angle at Alexandria he could calculate the polar circumference of the Earth.

Original units of measurement

When we look at ancient structures and the sacred geometry embodied within them we should think as the original builders did and work with the units of measurement they used rather than with our modern units.

When they were setting out the building's dimensions, the original designers of sacred structures and temples often used units consisting of whole numbers that had a magical quality. For example, the height of the Great Pyramid, Egypt, is 481.654 feet (146.808 m) with a base of 765.8756 feet (233.439 m). How much clearer it becomes when we say it is 280 cubits high with a base of 440 cubits. By using the original whole numbers and simple fractions we can begin to analyse the sacred proportions and associated geometry embodied in these magnificent and enduring structures.

BELOW Painting of Egyptian men measuring distance using ropes and knots by P Marchandon de la Faye c.1879.

Understanding and accuracy

If we knew the original unit of measurement that was used to construct an ancient stone circle, such as Stonehenge, we could understand the structure in more depth. The inside diameter of a stone circle might read 97.3186 feet (29.663 m) on our modern decimal tape measure, but if we discovered the original unit of measurement we could say the diameter was a whole number, such as 36 megalithic yards. The figure 36 clearly says something about the symbolism of the circle, whereas 29.663 definitely does not.

ABOVE Where the capstone is missing from a pyramid, simple geometry can be used to calculate the height of the pyramid. Capstone from the pyramid of Ramose, scribe of the royal tomb of Rameses II, Egypt.

If original units of measurement are not easy to apply, a good alternative is to use ratios. A building, such as the Parthenon, Stonehenge or the Great Pyramid, can still be measured with modern metric units, but the ratios of the measurements can reveal more meaningful results. These ratios so often turn out to be simple whole-number fractions or 'magic numbers', such as the Golden Mean (see pages 34–39). A ratio, of course, is the same, no matter what units are used.

Finally, the use of original units of measurement gives us the chance to micro-correct faulty measurements and make them more accurate—by this I don't mean taking liberties with the figures. The stones of all ancient monuments have been damaged, moved or eroded, so even the best survey often cannot deduce the exact original length. If you measure 765.8756 feet (233.439 m) then you have no way of checking it, but a measure of 439.78 cubits is more than likely to have originally been 440 cubits exactly. So although I don't hold with tampering with the figures to get the 'right' answers, I do think that the use of original units of measurements can often point up very small discrepancies caused by the passage of time or the use of a limp tape measure.

The ancient root units of measurement

Why are units of measurement so important? In any culture there is a preference for round numbers, and this will often be a clue. A designer or architect is more likely to specify that something is 6.5616 feet (2 m) long rather than 6.385 feet (1.946 m) long: this is basic human nature.

For many structures—particularly religious or sacred ones—the choice of units for a dimension will not just be a whole number but often a magical or sacred number. A temple is more likely to be 60 or 64 units long rather than 63 units long, with subsidiary measurements in whole-number ratios (or $\sqrt{2}$ or $\sqrt{3}$) of the main dimensions. Why? Because our subconscious ideas of beauty, which we refer to as proportion, are dependent on proportional geometric division.

Much work has been devoted to discovering the ancient units of measurement so that we can draw plans of ancient structures in the original units, which show these key ratios. What were the ancient standards of length, weight and time? These are well documented in the case of the Roman or Greek foot, but

ABOVE Castlerigg Stone Circle, which may date back to 3200 BC, near Keswick, England, showing some of its 38 standing stones, which form a circle 36 megalithic yards across.

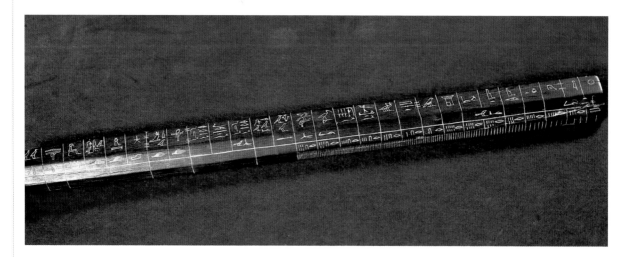

ABOVE **An Egyptian ruler showing the detailed division of the cubit into fractions.**

in the case of pre-literate megalithic monuments we can only infer which unit was used by measuring many structures and correlating our findings. Two such ancient measures are the so-called megalithic yard and the cubit. The cubit is well documented, but the megalithic yard has been derived by retro-fitting.

The megalithic yard

Although it initially seems unlikely, the evidence suggests that a uniform system of measurement extended across a wide variety of cultures. Researchers, including Professor Alexander Thom and John Michell, have concluded that one particular unit of measurement was used by the ancient architects of megalithic structures across much of Europe.

The original measurements were often very accurate, and it stands to reason that megalithic sites would be carefully surveyed and planned before such huge stones were moved considerable distances to make the structure. Thom called this theoretic unit of measurement used on the megalithic sites the megalithic yard and equated it with 2.717 feet (0.8296 m).

We have to be careful not to allow modern thinking to color our view of the past. Although the French devisers of the meter defined it in terms of the circumference of the Earth, we cannot therefore assume that our predecessors had necessarily hit upon the same idea. So, for example, Michael Behrend (author of *The Landscape Geometry of Southern Britain*, a monograph) in 1976 suggested that an ancient unit used by megalithic surveyors (968.9 feet or 295.32 m) was formed from the equatorial radius of the Earth divided by 6 x 60 x 60, derived from just six measurements.

The difficulty with such statements is that even if our remote ancestors knew the precise diameter or circumference of the Earth, would they have necessarily used it as a measurement baseline? I think not. With such a difference in magnitude between the Earth's dimensions and a unit ruler, it is always easy to figure out or fudge a suitable ratio. The Greeks had already worked out the circumference of the Earth (see pages 26–27), but their standard of measurement predated that discovery by some considerable time.

I doubt if any civilization, except the French, ever based its units of measurement on a calculation of the Earth's circumference. Units were derived from immediately observable and common things such as the (standardized) length of an arm or the weight of a wheat seed. The only system to have started from what it thought to be the size of the Earth was the French metric system, and they got this original measurement wrong anyway.

A more fruitful approach has been employed by the authors of *Civilization One*, Christopher Knight and Alan Butler. They appear to have discovered that surprisingly many apparently modern systems of measurement have probably been derived from the original megalithic yard. This seems a more promising route, and so I have modified their approach slightly to use the megalithic yard, which almost miraculously provides many sites with whole numbers for their key dimensions, and consequently in many cases magical or sacred numbers appear with much greater than statistical regularity. The value for this megalithic yard is 2.717 feet (0.8296 m) = 32.661 inches (82.96 cm).

The cubit

In the Middle East the standard has always been the cubit, a measure dependent on the length of an adult man's forearm. There are, however, two different cubits—the royal and the standard. Each royal cubit was divided into seven smaller units called palms, which corresponded to the width of a hand. A standard cubit was divided into six palms. These two measures were used for different types of structures so their difference never

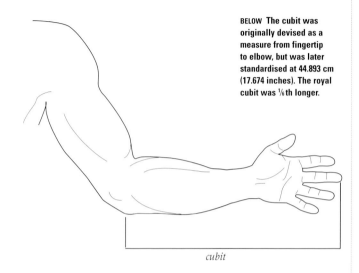

cubit

became a problem. The palm was further subdivided into four fingers, giving 24 or 28 fingers per cubit, both eminently divisible numbers. Because body sizes varied, the Egyptians standardized their cubits. We would define these as:

Royal cubit = 20.620 inches
= 52.375 cm

Standard cubit = 17.674 inches
= 44.892 cm

We know these to be absolutely precise because the Egyptians had standardized metal rulers showing these divisions and so there is no question of miscalculation.

The megalithic yard was, however, not directly related to the cubit, as much as our sense of neatness might like it to be.

palm

ABOVE The palm is equal to the width of four fingers. Six palms make up one cubit and seven palms make up a royal cubit.

The curious nature of prime numbers

Prime numbers are rather mysterious, and to this day mathematicians have tried in vain to discover some order in their sequence. Prime numbers grow erratically, like weeds, among the composite numbers. They seem to obey no other law than that of chance and no one has so far been able to predict where the next one will appear.

In other ways prime numbers exhibit stunning regularity and satisfy many strange and wonderful properties. In fact, primes are very important commercially—programmers are constantly striving to devise prime factorization algorithms that can generate the prime factors of any given integer. A fundamental theorem states that any positive integer can be represented in exactly one way as a product of primes. Many of the commercial banking and Internet codes we use today depend upon the difficulty of factorizing primes. If someone were able to devise a general method of factoring primes, they would render the vast majority of encryption schemes in current use easily breakable. So you can see that the arithmetic of prime numbers is not just a Pythagorean pastime but serious business.

What is a prime number?
A prime number is a positive integer that has no positive divisors other than 1 and itself. For example, the only divisors of 13 are 1 and 13, making 13 a prime number. The number 24 has many divisors (1, 2, 3, 4, 6, 8, 12, and 24), which means 24 is not a prime number. Positive integers that are not prime are called composite numbers. Prime numbers are, therefore, numbers that cannot be factored, and they may in a sense be considered the building blocks of all composite numbers.

The number 1 is a special case and is considered to be neither prime nor composite. With 1 excluded, the smallest prime is therefore 2. However, since 2 is the only even prime, it may also be excluded from the list of primes.

BELOW Peter Plichta's prime number circle, showing their regular irregularity.

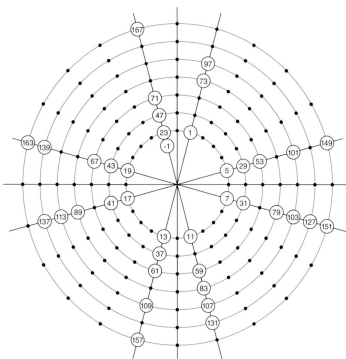

Prime number signatures

We know that the Ancients were fascinated by prime numbers and by fractions, so what about prime numbers used as the denominator of fractions? Let us try expanding some unitary prime fractions:

⅓ = 0.3333333333 ... (the same single number repeating).
⅕ = 0.2 (nothing interesting here).
1⁄7 = 0.142857 142857 142857 (the whole block of six numbers is repeating).
1⁄11 = 0.09 09 09 09 ... (just 09, a block of two numbers, repeating).
1⁄13 = 0.076923 076923 076923 ... (another block of six numbers repeating).

If we take just the 7ths we can develop this even further. You see the same group of six digits repeating endlessly but starting at a different point each time. It is almost as if *142857* was a sort of 'signature' of the prime number 7.

1⁄7 = 0.142857 142857 142857
2⁄7 = 0.2857 142857
3⁄7 = 0.42857 142857
4⁄7 = 0.57 142857 142857

Other signatures can be developed for other primes.

The sieve of Eratosthenes

Eratosthenes (*c.*275–194 BC) developed a sieve technique for discovering all the prime numbers. The procedure is as follows:

1 Sequentially write down the integers from 2 to the highest number, *n*, you wish to include in the table.

2 Cross out all numbers greater than 2 that are divisible by 2 (in other words, every second number), as they can never be primes. Find the smallest remaining number greater than 2. It is 3.

3 Cross out all numbers greater than 3 that are divisible by 3 (every third remaining number). Find the smallest remaining number greater than 3. It is 5.

4 Cross out all numbers greater than 5 that are divisible by 5 (every fifth remaining number).

Continue until you have crossed out all numbers divisible by $\sqrt{n}$ (the highest number you are interested in). The numbers remaining are primes.

The procedure in this example only needs to cross out primes up to $\sqrt{50}$, or 7, and no further.

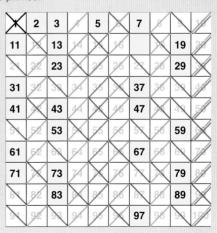

Prime numbers can be generated by the sieve of Eratosthenes (see box). The first few primes are 2, 3, 5, 7, 11, 13, 17, 19, 23, 29, 31, 37... The largest known prime so far discovered, as of February 2005, is the Mersenne prime of $2^{25964951} - 1$. However, there is no end in sight.

With the exception of 2 and 3, all primes are of the form $p = 6n +/- 1$. For example, for $n = 5$, the primes will be 29 and 31 (6 x 5, plus or minus 1 = 29 or 31.

The Golden Mean:
the arithmetic of growth

Johannes Kepler (1571–1630) called the Golden Section 'one of the two great treasures of geometry,' and it was likened by him rather poetically to a precious jewel. In the 16th century it was called the Divine Proportion and in the 19th century it was given the title Golden Number or Golden Ratio or Golden Section. We will call it the Golden Mean.

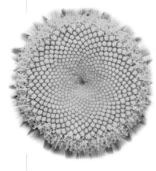

ABOVE The center of this daisy is an example of a natural form patterned on two interlocking spirals derived from the Fibonacci series.

The common Greek letter for the Golden Mean used to be *tau*, which comes from the Greek word 'to cut' or 'section'. Since the early 20th century it has been expressed as *phi*, Φ, which is the first letter of the name of the most famous Greek sculptor Phidias (490–430 BC), as a commemoration of its occurrence in various beautiful forms. We will later come to the use of Φ in various works of art, including its relatively minor use in the major work by Phidias, the Parthenon in Athens (see pages 124–127).

Creating the Golden Mean

Φ (*phi*) is a sacred number with a value of 1.6180339887… . It can be used to divide a line or rectangle into two unequal parts, so that the proportion of the two new parts is the same as the proportion of the larger part to the original line. Lateral thinking shows that division by this number is like cell division: the division of the line in this proportion causes the creation of another line proportionately identical to the original line. You could think of this produced line as the 'child' of the original line. The fact that Φ enables this process to continue indefinitely suggests its involvement in replication and hence in growth.

Let us do this division in a more formal way with the line AB:

$$A\text{————————}Y\text{———}B$$

Where

$$\frac{AY}{AB} = \frac{YB}{AY}$$

Cut it at Y into parts AY and YB. For these two parts to be illustrative of the Golden Mean, the ratio between AY and YB must be exactly the same as the ratio between AB and AY. This ratio is always 1.6180339887… to 1.

This decimal recurs forever, so its value cannot ever be expressed perfectly in decimal form. It is therefore an 'irrational number'. Irrational numbers are numbers that cannot be expressed by either an ending or a regularly repeating pattern of numbers after the decimal point. Another irrational number is *pi*, π (3.1415926 …). Even though it is an irrational number, Φ in its relationship with itself can form whole rational numbers. In geometry, it is an integral part of the generation of many polyhedra (see pages 56–57), and many sources show this as it is used extensively in nature to construct life forms.

Constructing a pentagon

The construction of a pentagon, if done by measurement rather than with a compass, relies on the formula:

Length of side of a regular pentagon inscribed in a circle of radius 1 unit.
$= \sqrt{(10 - 2\sqrt{5})}/2$

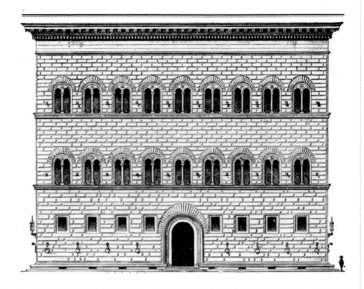

RIGHT The Palazzo Strozzi designed by Leon Battista Alberti and begun in 1489 in Florence, Italy, has one of the most regular and geometric plans governed by the canons of 15th-century architectural proportion.

How to construct the Golden Mean geometrically

To cut any target line into the Golden Mean proportions you can use the Pythagorean triangular method as follows:

1. Label the line AB.

2. Draw a line at right angles from B and label its end C—make this line half the length of the target line AB.

3. Draw a line connecting A and C. You have now constructed a Pythagorean right-angled triangle.

4. Put the point of a compass in C and, with radius CB, draw an arc cutting AC at point X.

5. Put the point of a compass in A and, with radius AX, draw an arc cutting AB at point Y. Y now divides the target line AB in the proportion of the Golden Mean.

1

2

3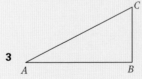

4

5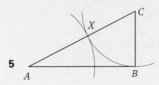

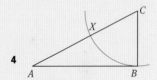
$$\frac{AY}{AB} \qquad \frac{YB}{AY}$$

Some Golden Mean (Φ) equations

Φ	$= (\sqrt{5} + 1)/2$	= 1.618
Φ²	$= (\sqrt{5} + 3)/2$	= 2.618
1/Φ	$= (\sqrt{5} - 1)/2$	= 0.618

From the above values we can say:

$$\Phi^2 = \Phi + 1$$
$$\Phi = \Phi^2 - 1$$
$$\Phi + \Phi^2 = \Phi^3$$
$$\Phi + \Phi^2 + \Phi^3 = \Phi^4$$

... and so on *ad infinitum*

Φ	= (cosecant 18°)/2
	= 1/(2 sine 18°)
	= 2 cosine 36°
	= 2/(secant 36°)
	= 2 sine 54°
	= 2/(cosecant 54°)
	= (secant 72°)/2
	= 1/(2 cosine 72°)

From inspecting the above, you can see that 18, 36, 54 and 72 are key numbers. Now, as these are all multiples of 18, this number is intimately associated with **Φ**.

As we have seen, the Ancients always preferred numbers that could be expressed as whole numbers or fractions (such as ⅔, ½, ¼, ⅛) and preferably unitary fractions, which are fractions with 1 as the numerator (such as ⅓, ⅙, ¹⁄₁₀).

So here is *phi* expressed as a fraction:

$$\Phi = (1 + \sqrt{5})/2$$

We can reduce the equation to a simpler form by dividing through by 2:

$$\Phi = 0.5 + (\sqrt{5} \times 0.5)$$

Φ is now expressed entirely in terms of 5, so it should not come as a surprise that 'fiveness' is a quality of Φ and that Φ occurs in the proportions of the pentagon (a five-sided figure) and of the pentagram (a five-pointed figure).

Incommensurate numbers

However, in its decimal form *phi* never ends. Numbers that are never-ending, and cannot be exactly expressed, are called incommensurate where they cannot be constructed with basic Euclidean geometry using a compass and a straightedge.

They have intrigued man since antiquity. One rather florid story relates that when Hippasus of Metapontum (*c.*500 BC) discovered that the Golden Mean can never be expressed as a fraction or a ratio between two whole numbers, his fellow Pythagoreans were so shocked they were said to have sacrificed 100 oxen. I think this is probably an exaggeration, given that Pythagoreans were vegetarians, but it shows the degree of their veneration for whole numbers and their rational relationships as expressed as rational fractions.

Iamblichus of Chalcis (AD 245–325) stated that the Pythagoreans built a tomb for whoever discovered incommensurability, signifying that he must forever depart from the life and fellowship of Pythagorean society.

The Golden Triangle

The Golden or Sublime Triangle is an isosceles triangle with both base angles of 72 degrees and the third angle of 36 degrees. When the base angles are bisected (cut in half) the two new triangles produced are also Golden

The geometry of a pentagram

A regular pentagram circumscribed by a circle consists of an inverted pentagon plus five triangles. Each of these triangles, like CKD in the illustration, is a Golden Triangle because they each have base angles of 72 degrees and a vertex angle of 36 degrees. If you take their sides as 1 unit, their base is 0.618 ... units long, or to put it another way, the ratio of the side to the base is Φ or 1.618 ... .

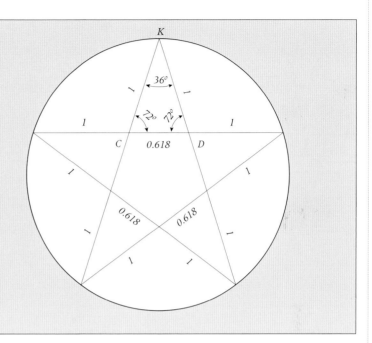

Triangles. This process can be repeated over and over, each time creating new Golden Triangles in the same way you can continue producing Golden Rectangles.

The Golden Triangle also produces the Golden Mean of 1.618, because the ratio between the longer side and the short side of the triangle is *phi*, as the illustration above shows. This triangle can also be used to produce a type of logarithmic spiral (see pages 48–51).

The Golden Pentagram

The pentagram, or five-pointed star, has long been considered magical. In the West it is often used specifically as a protection against evil, with the single point upwards. When the double point is upwards the pentagram is construed as an evil sign. The most famous magical fraternity of the last few centuries, the

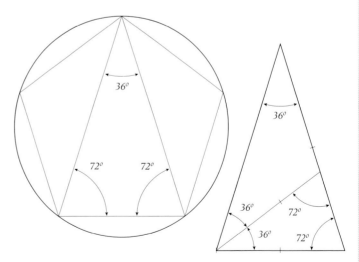

ABOVE One Golden Triangle may be constructed on each of the five sides of a regular pentagon. The Golden Triangle has both base angles of 72 degrees, which can be bisected to form another Golden Triangle and so on forever.

Hermetic Order of the Golden Dawn, used it to devise a Banishing Ritual of the Pentagram to help disperse undesirable entities. It is therefore not surprising that this figure also has some special geometry.

If you look closely at the pentagram, you will see that it is made up of five triangles attached to an upside-down regular pentagon.

If the sides of the five triangular points are one unit in length, then the base of these triangles (or the side of the pentagon) is 0.618. Interestingly, 1/0.618 is Φ. Or, to put it yet another way, if you divide the sides of the triangle by the base of the triangle you get Φ. In short the regular pentagon is made up of five Golden Triangles, touching each other around a pentagon.

Fibonacci and his miraculous series

Although Leonardo da Vinci is world famous, it is another Leonardo who contributed one of the main discoveries that lie at the heart of sacred geometry.

In 1202 Leonardo of Pisa or Fibonacci (c.1170–c.1240) published his *Liber abaci*

'The Book of Calculations'. In its 15 chapters he explained the basic operations of arithmetic, especially the theory of prime numbers, fractions and Euclid. Then, only as a minor mathematical diversion, almost an afterthought, he came up with the idea of the Fibonacci series.

Leonardo of Pisa had the reputation of bringing the mathematical arts from Arabia to Italy, in other words, translating key mathematical texts from Arabic into Latin. He collected these during his extensive travels to traditional centers of learning, including Egypt, Syria, Greece, Sicily, and Provence. Sicily (together with Toledo) played an especially important role in the transmission of Arabic science to the West as it had been captured by the Saracens in 827, before the Norman knights drove them out between 1060 and 1092. The result, in Leonardo of Pisa's lifetime, was a good mixture of Greek, Latin and Arabic culture and knowledge

The very root of beauty

Dan Brown works the Fibonacci series into his *The Da Vinci Code* right at the beginning, as the sequence scrawled on

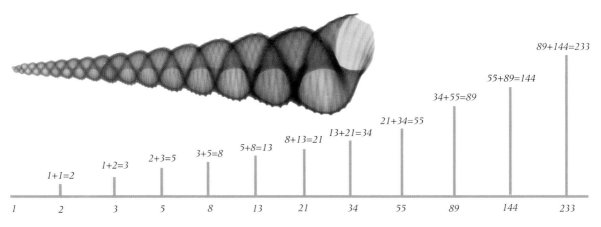

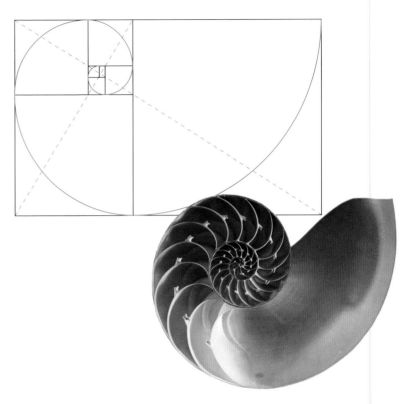

the floor by the dying curator Sauniere, and later by using it as a code in the bank deposit box security number. Leonardo of Pisa originated it as part of a mathematical diversion designed to calculate the course of a burgeoning rabbit population, assuming certain reproductory rules, beginning with a single pair of rabbits. The resulting number of rabbits at each generation was:

1, 1, 2, 3, 5, 8, 13, 21, 34, 55, 89, 144 …

Each term is the sum of the previous two terms, so the series effectively 'grows' by always referring back to its immediately previous 'parent' numbers. It is an ordinary-looking series until you start to examine the relationship between each number and its successor. This grows more interesting if you divide each number by its immediate predecessor (rounded to three decimal places):

$\frac{3}{2}$	=	1.500
$\frac{5}{3}$	=	1.666
$\frac{8}{5}$	=	1.600
$\frac{13}{8}$	=	1.625
$\frac{21}{13}$	=	1.615
$\frac{34}{21}$	=	1.619
$\frac{55}{34}$	=	1.617
$\frac{89}{55}$	=	1.618

Each successive division dodges around a bit, then stabilizes to become 1.6180339887… . This magic number has been expressed by the Greek letter *phi*, Φ, (see page 34). This piece of arithmetic relates directly to an interesting example of geometry. Using the ratio 1 and 1.618 to form the sides of a rectangle makes it become a Golden Rectangle that is derived

from the Golden Mean. It has long been recognized that the number *phi*, Φ, is definitely part of the underlying structure of the universe and can therefore rightly be called 'sacred'.

The ancient Greek and Renaissance architects very effectively used *phi* as a way of establishing some of the most visually pleasing ratios for the dimensions of a building, even sometimes down to the proportion of individual windows and doors. You need only to compare a building from either of those two periods with, say, a piece of modern architecture produced in Britain during the 1960s to arbitrary and 'socially conscious' dimensions to realize that Φ is more than just an arithmetical concept—it is part of the very root of beauty.

ABOVE The shells of the nautilus and the ammonite adopt the same geometric form, spiralling out at an ever increasing rate that is governed by this geometry.

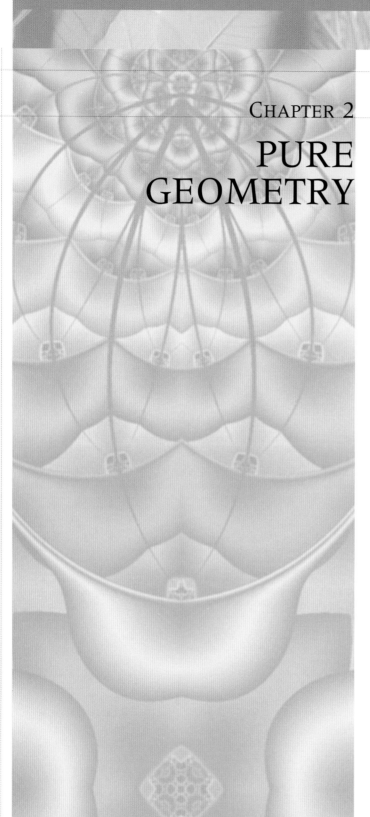

CHAPTER 2

PURE GEOMETRY

Greek geometers, the greatest of whom was Euclid, saw the perfection of geometry as a reflection of the mind of the creator. To further distance geometry from the physical world, they used only a straightedge (not a ruler with marked divisions) and a compass to draw and prove their theorems.

After exploring the most basic figures (the circle and the four key types of triangle) we look at the three classic geometric problems: the squaring of the circle, the duplication of the cube and the trisection of an angle.

Of all the possible 3-D figures, only five (Plato's solids) were considered perfect, while a further 13 (associated with Archimedes) were also important. In addition, the Greeks also discovered the fascinating properties of the cone and conceived a number of curves, including the logarithmic curve, which plays such a large part in the geometry of life.

The Greek geometers devised geometric figures that embodied the irrational numbers, which were looked upon with horror because of their supposed imperfection. These numbers, particularly the square roots of 2, 3 and 5, play a big part in sacred geometry as they often form the length of diagonals of squares and rectangles made from small whole numbers.

Euclid: the father of geometry

Euclid (325–265 BC), who is known as the father of geometry, is responsible for assembling almost all the world's knowledge of flat-plane and 3-D geometry in one book. His work, together with the work of Pythagoras, forms the basis of all sacred geometry. It is only in the last few centuries that any new and significant geometry has been added to what Euclid laid down 2,300 years ago.

ABOVE Euclid, considered the father of geometry, was the author of the only body of scientific knowledge that has remained valid and unchanged for more than two millennia.

The best-known book in the history of geometry, or indeed the whole of mathematics, is *Elements* by Euclid. Only the Bible has sold more copies in Europe, at least until the 20th century brought us huge bestsellers such as *The Lord of the Rings*, *The Da Vinci Code* and the book series about Hogwarts and Harry Potter.

Euclid probably first studied mathematics in Athens with some of Plato's students. He also wrote almost a dozen other books on topics, such as music, mechanics and optics, although only four survive. One of them, *Optics*, contains some of the earliest studies of perspective (see pages 142–143).

Theon of Alexandria wrote a revised version of *Elements* in the fourth century AD and this served as the basis of all translations until the 19th century, when a manuscript containing a somewhat different text was discovered in the Vatican Library. In the Middle Ages *Elements* was translated into Arabic at least three times. An English Benedictine monk, Adelard of Bath (*c.*1070–1145), who was traveling in Spain disguised as a Muslim student, acquired an Arabic text of *Elements* and completed the translation into Latin around 1120. This translation became the basis of all editions in Europe until the 16th century when, in 1570, Sir Henry Billingsley translated *Elements* into English. Dr John Dee (see pages 93–95) wrote the preface and considered that a basic knowledge of Euclid would be of great advantage in the study of optics and in building and architecture.

The great Greek geometers

The ancient Greeks were interested in the elegant solution of a geometric problem for its own sake. Their geometry has underpinned the calculations of harmony that go to make up sacred geometry, and its step-by-step logic is the basis of modern scientific reasoning. They created ideals of classical beauty (especially sculpture), stunning architecture (via the Greek and Roman Renaissance) and the logical scientific approach to solving problems. These ideals of beauty were accompanied by a knowledge of form and proportion that are the bedrock of sacred geometry.

Euclid codified geometry and Pythagoras explained the inherent sacredness of numbers, but many Greek geometers helped to build the strong foundations of architecture, astronomy, mechanics and optics, and their work is still at the heart of Western science today.

ABOVE Directional compass with inbuilt sundial, which is calibrated to work accurately at several different latitudes.

Euclid's *Elements*

The 13 books of *Elements* encompass most of the geometric knowledge of Euclid's time. They contains almost all we know about plane (flat surface) geometry and much that we know about the geometry of spheres, cones and other 3-D figures. Euclidean geometry needs only a compass and a straightedge. A ruler with marked divisions is not strictly necessary because Euclid's theorems work regardless of scale. The following checklist of the books of *Elements* will help locate the source of many of Euclid's more important theorems and ideas:

Books I to **IV** deal with the plane geometry we learn in school and that has become known as Euclidean geometry. Books I, II and IV discuss lines and plane figures, while Book III presents theorems related to the circle.
Book V gives an extensive account of the work on proportion that originated with Eudoxus of Cnidus (*c*.408–355 BC). This volume is of particular importance to the study of sacred geometry.
Books VII to **IX** deal with number theory and the foundations of arithmetic, and of these Book VII is the most relevant for the study of numbers *per se*.
Book X elaborates on irrational numbers and is mostly derived from the work of Theaetetus of Athens (417–369 BC).
Book XI provides the basis for solid 3-D geometry.
Book XII proves the theorem for the area of the circle and is mostly derived from the work of Eudoxus.
Book XIII demonstrates the construction of the five Platonic solids and is mostly derived from the work of Theaetetus. This volume is also of particular importance to sacred geometry.

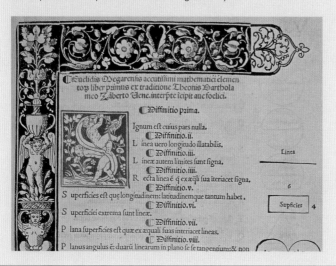

Plato (427–347 BC)

Thales of Miletus (624–546 BC)
Sometimes called the 'father of deductive reasoning', Thales was one of the first to bring the science of geometry from Egypt to Greece—three centuries before Euclid.

Plato (427–347 BC)
Plato founded an Academy in 387 BC that flourished until AD 529. Plato's book *Phaedo* supported Pythagoras by attempting to prove that numbers and figures are the perfect noumenal forms behind manifested reality.

Theaetetus of Athens (417–369 BC)
He created the solid geometry of the five Platonic solids (see pages 54–55), and his work fascinated Renaissance writers on proportion and sacred geometry.

Eudoxus of Cnidus (408–355 BC)
His work inspired Book V of Euclid's *Elements* and deals with proportion and harmony, which became key factors in Greek architecture and sacred geometry. Eudoxus also devised methods for determining the area of circles and the volumes of pyramids and cones.

Menaechmus (380–320 BC)
He was the first geometer to demonstrate that ellipses, parabolas and hyperbolas can

all be obtained simply by cutting a cone obliquely at different points. Kepler used his work to determine the elliptical orbits of the planets (see pages 78–79).

Archimedes (c.287–212 BC)

He formalized the geometry of simple devices by comparing the radius of a curve with the angle made with its origin, which is the key to understanding logarithmic curves (see pages 48–51). Archimedes discovered 13 semi-regular, 3-D solids (see pages 56–57).

Apollonius of Perga (262–190 BC)

Apart from calculating a better approximation for *pi* than Archimedes, Apollonius' main contribution to geometry was the calculation of the centre of curvature and the original curve (evolute) of the ellipse, parabola (see pages 48–51) and hyperbola.

Hipparchus of Rhodes (190–120 BC)

He published the first trigonometric tables and may even have invented trigonometry. Interestingly, the tables were based on dividing a circle into

Hipparchus of Rhodes (190–120 BC)

360 degrees (for the first time), with each degree divided into 60 minutes—an idea he borrowed from the Babylonians.

Heron of Alexandria (AD 10–75)

Heron worked on both plane figures and the surfaces of 3-D objects. He worked out how to divide areas and volumes according to a given ratio, part of which involved finding the cube root of a number.

Menelaus of Alexandria (AD 70–130)

He applied spherical geometry to astronomy and so opened the way to more sophisticated astronomical calculations.

Claudius Ptolemy (AD 85–165)

Ptolemy wrote the *Almagest* (13 books), which remained the standard work on astronomy until his theories were overturned by Copernicus and Kepler (see pages 75–79). He provided the essential mathematics for the geocentric theory of planetary motion.

Pappus of Alexandria (AD 290–350)

Pappus' work included proportionals, geometric paradoxes, regular solids, the spiral, the quadratrix, trisection, honeycombs, semi-regular solids, minimal surfaces, astronomy, and mechanics. He also devised the basis of modern projective geometry used in map making.

Hypatia of Alexandria (AD 370–415)

The daughter of Theon of Alexandria, Hypatia embodied the connection between philosophy and geometry. She edited a new version of Euclid's *Elements* and, in about AD 400, became head of the last Platonist school at Alexandria.

Archimedes (c.287–212 BC)

Three key triangles

Triangles are one of the fundamental figures in geometry. There are millions of possible triangles, but we will focus on just three: right-angled, equilateral and isosceles triangles. These special triangles form some of the building blocks of sacred geometry and have been used at different times in the construction of sacred buildings.

The most basic element in geometry is a point. When two points are connected a straight line forms. Curved lines create figures such as a circle, ellipse and parabola.

Two straight lines create an angle, which is measured in degrees and minutes using a sexagesimal notation—counting based on 60s—which the Babylonians invented thousands of years ago. It is infinitely more flexible in handling fractions than the base 10 system we use today. The Babylonians divided the circle into 360 degrees, each degree into 60 minutes and each minute into 60 seconds. This means that they could achieve a precision to 1 part in 1.3 million (as 360 x 60 x 60 = 1,296,000).

A straight line has an angle of 180 degrees. Three straight lines linked together create a triangle—a three-angled and three-sided figure that is perhaps the most stable figure in all of geometry. Because of its stability it was used for triangulation in land surveying and mapping. The triangle owes its stability to the fact that the sum of its three internal angles always equals 180 degrees, exactly half a full circle.

Right-angled triangles

The distinguishing feature of a right-angled triangle is that it has one angle of 90 degrees. The remaining two angles can be any value (even 1 degree and 89 degrees) as long as the sum of all three angles adds up to 180 degrees. The formula that links the length the three sides is Pythagoras' Theorem (see page 17). The right-angled triangle is crucial to constructing a building or mapping a field.

A specific example is the 3,4,5 right-angled triangle, which the ancient

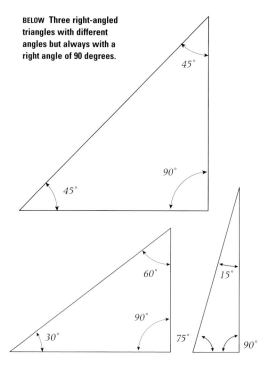

BELOW **Three right-angled triangles with different angles but always with a right angle of 90 degrees.**

45°

90°

45°

60°

90°

30°

15°

75°

90°

Egyptians used to lay out their fields. A rope with 12 knots, marking 12 units of equal length, was strung tight to form a perfect right-angled triangle, with sides of 3 + 4 + 5 = 12 units.

Another example is the so-called Great Pyramid triangle (see pages 117–119), a special triangle, which has sides of 1, √Φ (1.273 ...) and Φ (1.618).

Equilateral triangles

The next most important triangle is the equilateral triangle, which has sides of the same length and angles of the same size (60 degrees), no matter how long the sides are. Six equilateral triangles placed side by side will fit into a complete circle (6 x 60 = 360) and will make a hexagon.

Isosceles triangles

The third type of triangle is the isosceles triangle, which has two equal angles and two sides of equal length (the ones opposite the equal angles). An example might have internal angles of 35 degrees, 35 degrees and 110 degrees. A special example of this is the Golden Triangle (see pages 36–37), which has angles of 72 degrees, 72 degrees and 36 degrees.

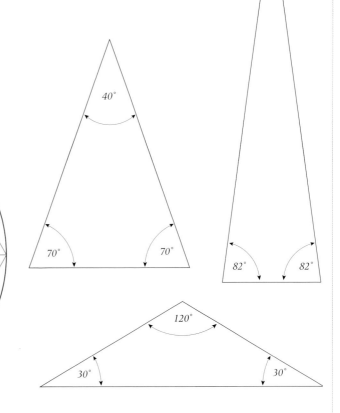

ABOVE An equilateral triangle is used to generate a regular hexagram. All of the triangle's internal angles are 60 degrees.

ABOVE The isosceles triangle is distinguished by two features: two equal sides and two equal base angles.

Three ancient geometrical problems

Squaring the circle, duplicating a cube and trisecting an angle are three famous geometrical problems that puzzled the Ancients. Solving these problems had to be accomplished with only a compass and a straightedge.

Squaring the circle

This problem arose because of the need to calculate the area of a circle. The solution was to find a formula or geometric construction that would enable someone easily to draw a square with an area that exactly corresponded to the area of a particular circle. The difficulty of this problem has led many people to use the phrase 'squaring the circle' as a euphemism for something that was almost impossible yet mystical.

The ancient Egyptians identified certain pairs of whole numbers (8 and 9 are most often quoted) that came fairly close to squaring the circle. A circle with a diameter of 9 units (any unit) almost corresponds in area to a square with sides of 8 units:

Area of circle = πr^2 = 22/7 x 4.5 x 4.5
= 63.64 square units
Area of square = 8 x 8
= 64 square units

Nearly correct, but still 0.56 per cent out. The ratio 8:9 is interesting because it corresponds to the second musical note or D (see pages 22–23).

In 1872, the German mathematician Ferdinand von Lindemann (1852–1939) proved that π was a transcendental number, finally showing that it was not possible to square the circle using only a compass and a straightedge.

However, one of the other close approximations to circle squaring involves constructing a square with sides of 3.14164. This number is calculated from: 6 (1 + Φ)/5 = 3.141640.

This is particularly interesting as it shows there is an *almost* exact relationship between π(3.1415925) and Φ (the Golden Mean, or 1.618).

Doubling a cube

The second problem was how to produce a cube that was exactly double the volume of another cube. At first sight you might be inclined simply to double the length of each side, but this results in a volume 2 x 2 x 2 = 8 times the original volume.

The solution involves using cube roots, which by their very nature cannot be constructed with purely Euclidean geometry. This problem is also extremely practical as it relates to the construction of standard measuring devices for liquids and grain. It was also a key to constructing the Parthenon—double the volume of the previous temple (see pages 124–127).

RIGHT The simplest near squaring of the circle is the ratio of 9:8 where the circle is 9 units in diameter and the square has sides of 8 units.

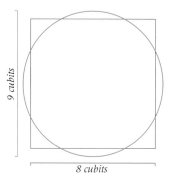

9 cubits

8 cubits

The problem can be solved algebraically. If the original cube has a side S long its volume will be S^3. Therefore, a cube with double the volume of this cube is equal to $2S^3$. So one side of the new cube will $= \sqrt{(2S^3)} = S \sqrt[3]{2} = S \times 1.26$.

Trisecting an angle

The third problem involves dividing an angle into three equal angles without using a protractor. Certain angles, such as 135 degrees or 90 degrees, can be trisected using a compass and straightedge, but very few others.

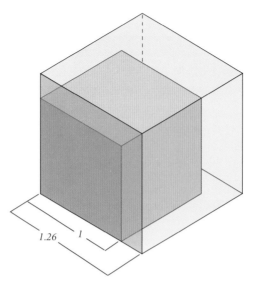

The quadratrix

The Greek philosopher Hippias of Elis (*c.*460–*c.*400 BC) provided the closest solution to two of these three geometrical problems when he discovered the curve called the quadratrix. This curve is generated inside a square (in the diagram ABCD).

Imagine using A as a 'hinge' so that the side AD collapses down in a circular path DFB until it coincides with AB. In so doing it inscribes DFB an arc of a circle. At the same time, imagine a horizontal (dotted) line descending at the same rate from DC to AB. As these two motions happen in sync, so their intersection point moves along the line DXG. This line DXYG is the quadratrix. Its formula is: x = y cotangent (y × π/2).

Consider the right angle DAB. To solve the problem of trisecting an angle, simply draw one of the dotted lines one-third of the way down the square. By drawing a line from A to the point where this dotted line cuts the quadratrix, you have drawn a line that has

created an angle one-third of the whole angle DAB. Likewise, if the dotted line is two-thirds down the square, the angle formed DAY will be two-thirds of DAB.

To draw an angle BAZ, one-sixth of angle DAB, use the dotted line AZ (see right)

The quadratrix can also be used to produce an almost rigorous squaring of the circle.

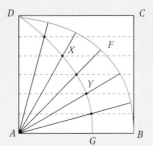

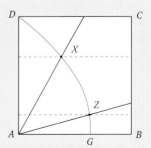

Curves and logarithmic spirals

A circle is said to be a perfect image of God, but it is also closed and static.
By contrast, a spiral is a dramatic image of life, with a starting point yet
no closure and no end, so it can extend itself forever. It is the irrepressible
force of life or, as the poet Dylan Thomas put it, 'the force that through the
green fuse drives the flower.'

Logarithmic spirals

What all spirals have in common is expansion and growth. There are many types of spiral: flat spirals, 3-D spirals, right-handed spirals, left-handed spirals, equi-angular spirals, geometric spirals, logarithmic spirals and rectangular spirals.

3-D spirals are made when a spiral winds around another geometric shape, such as a cone or cylinder, producing helix forms or helices like the DNA molecule (see pages 72–73).

A logarithmic or equi-angular spiral is generated when *phi* (the Golden Mean) is used as its key number. The logarithmic spiral is formed by means of 'whirling squares' growing in *phi*-controlled harmonic progression from the center outwards. This is best demonstrated by finding out yourself what happens geometrically (see page 49).

It is interesting to note that as logarithmic spirals increase in size by a geometric rate, the radii drawn from the centre to a point on the spiral form a geometric progression. The logarithmic spiral is the only curve that does not alter its shape as it grows.

The logarithmic spiral was later studied by that arch-logician René Descartes (1596–1650) and the mathematician Jakob Bernoulli (1654–1705). Bernoulli realized the spiral held the potential for growth and so requested one be engraved on his tombstone, together with the words *eadem mutata resurgo* (I shall arise transmuted).

Classic curves

The most important curve is the circle, but there are a number of other classic curves that were known and used by the Ancients. However, some of these curves have yet to be recognized as part of nature or sacred geometry.

Parabola

The parabola is a curve with fascinating properties. For example, a room with

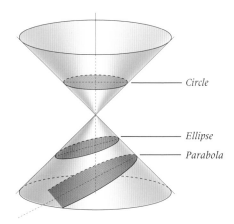

ABOVE The three classic curves, the circle, ellipse and parabola, are generated by cutting a cone at different angles.

Circle

Ellipse

Parabola

Constructing a logarithmic spiral

1 Start with a square with sides of one unit (be it inches, centimetres or whatever, it does not matter) and call it ABCD. Mark the midpoint of DA with an X (see diagram 1).

2 Anchor the compass at X and, with radius BX, drawn an arc. It will cut DA extended at point E. Use point E to construct a new rectangle, EFBA (see diagram 1). This construction produces a Golden Rectangle EFCD, and has resulted in several magical results. For example, DE is now cut by A in the Golden Mean proportion.

3 If you now draw the diagonals BE and DF they will always meet at right angles (see diagram 2). This is why the particular logarithmic spiral generated from this is called a right-angled logarithmic spiral.

4 Now take the long side, DE, of the Golden Rectangle just created and add the square HEDG. Continue adding squares, each time taking the long side of the Golden Rectangle just produced – HF, JC, LG and NI – to produce new Golden Rectangles, HFCG, IJCG, IKLG, IKMN and PKMO respectively (diagram 3)

5 Finally, draw by hand a smooth curve that joins the outer corners of each successively added square. The squares 'whirl' outwards, but each time keep the Golden Mean proportion (diagram 3).

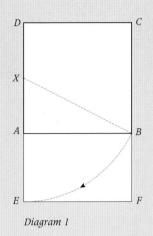

Diagram 1

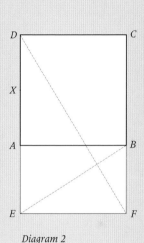

Diagram 2

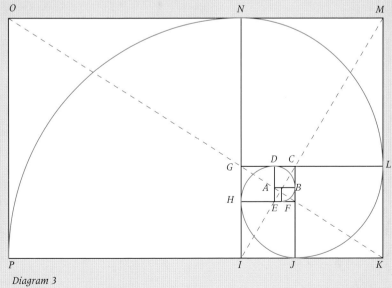

Diagram 3

parabolic-shaped walls at either end will transmit the sound of a whispered conversation from the focus of one parabola to the focus of the other, even though there are other noises. Such rooms can be found in the Exploratorium in San Francisco in California and the Statutary Hall in the US House of Representatives, Washington, D.C.

Ellipse

The ellipse is important because it is the geometric figure that governs the orbits of the planets round the Sun. Although the Greek geometers knew of the ellipse, Johannes Kepler (1571–1630) was the first to apply it to the orbit of the planets.

Lune

The lune is a moon-shaped figure that is bounded by two intersecting circles of different radii. Hippocrates of Chios (460–380 BC) investigated lunes as a possible (but unsuccessful) means of squaring the circle (see page 46).

ABOVE **If you look at the outer curve of an eagle's beak you will see that it forms a perfect involute curve.**

Involute

This natural curve can be seen in the curve of an eagle's beak, the dorsal fin of a shark and the tip of some palm fronds. It is best understood as the curve made by a rope as it unwinds from a cylinder.

Cycloid

The cycloid is a curve produced by a cylinder as it rolls across a flat surface—it has therefore been know for a very long time. As the cylinder rolls, it produces a long, beautiful curve, which can be used in arches and other constructions.

In the 17th century, many mathematicians and philosophers, including Galileo, Pascal, Descartes, Leibniz and Newton, fell under the spell of the cycloid. It was called 'the Helen of geometry', and its beauty includes the following fascinating facts:

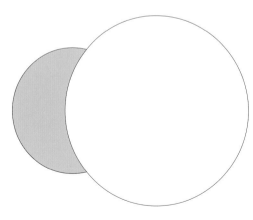

ABOVE **The lune, which is formed by the intersection of two circles with different diameters, is named after the crescent moon, which it resembles.**

• The cycloid's length is precisely four times the diameter of the circle that produces it—a very rational number.

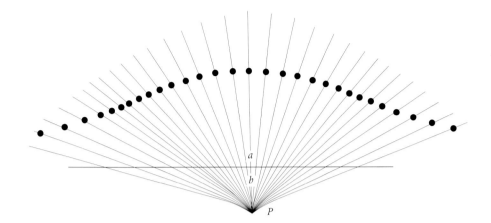

LEFT The conchoid of
Nicomedes, invented
*c.*200 BC, can be used to
trisect angles. The curve
is shown by the dots.

• The area under the arch of any cycloid is exactly three times the area of the rotating circle that makes it.
• The cycloid is a very rational figure, which is produced from a circle whose dimensions are themselves irrational (because *pi* is irrational).

Conchoid
The Greek mathematician Nicomedes (*c.*200 BC) is said to have discovered the conchoid curve and to have used it to solve two of the classic problems that straightedged Euclidean geometry could not—duplicating a cube and trisecting an angle (see pages 46–47).

A conchoid has the shape of a shell and is constructed by the interaction between a fixed line and a fixed point. Call the fixed point P and draw a series of rays from P so that they cross the fixed line. As you draw different rays, the distance from P to the line will change. You need to be aware of the length of these rays on the same side as P, as compared with their length on the opposite side of the line.

As you draw each ray you must use a rule to determine just how long each will be, and in so doing, just how far each ray will project beyond the fixed line. The conchoid is the curve that joins up all the ends of the rays.

BELOW The cycloid is formed by plotting a point on the rim of a wheel rolling along a flat plane. It was first defined in 1501 by Charles Bouvelles.

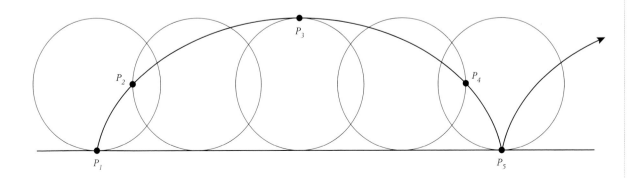

The geometry of irrational numbers

For modern mathematicians irrational numbers are those that cannot be pinned down to a few digits. They are, in fact, repeating decimals that go on forever. Examples include √2, √3 and √5. √1 and √4 are not included because they are the whole numbers 1 and 2 respectively. But for the Ancients they were most useful numbers.

ABOVE/RIGHT The use of knotted ropes was a common Egyptian method of rapidly fixing surveying triangles.

The Ancients used triangles to survey the land, a method of surveying called 'triangulation' that is still in use today. This is based on the fact that it is a difficult to mark out an exact rectangle over a large area of land and to make the corners exactly 90 degrees. Often, over a large area, you will finish up instead with a 'wobbly' parallelogram.

However, a triangle is much more foolproof, because once you establish one side of the triangle, the other two can meet at only one point. If you take this further and use three lengths of knotted cord (as the ancient Egyptians did) you can rapidly mark out a triangle from a baseline, with very little chance of error.

One trick, however, is to mark out a right-angled triangle. Then, using two such triangles, you can create a perfect rectangle, which is important if you are trying to survey the land accurately and avoid endless territorial disputes. The Egyptians often had to resurvey the land yearly, after each Nile inundation had obliterated the old field markers, and so they became experts at it.

Long before Pythagoras, the Egyptians knew that triangles with sides comprised of certain numbers (such as 3, 4, 5 or 17, 144, 145) would always create a right-angled triangle. These special whole numbers were later called Pythagorean

Triplets. Their surveying ropes were knotted in such a way as to produce triangles of sides that were always Pythagorean Triplets or generators of right-angled triangle. Of course, not every triangle was so convenient in its lengths, and right-angled triangle that were not composed of a Pythagorean Triplet combination always produced an irrational hypotenuse, or long side.

Calculating the hypotenuse

Let us look at some simple examples, using Pythagoras' theorem (see page 17) to work out the hypotenuse each time.

side 1	side 2	hypotenuse
1	1	$\sqrt{(1^2 + 1^2)} = \sqrt{(1 + 1)} = \sqrt{2}$ (irrational)
1	2	$\sqrt{(1^2 + 2^2)} = \sqrt{(1 + 4)} = \sqrt{5}$ (irrational)
3	4	$\sqrt{(3^2 + 4^2)} = \sqrt{(9 + 16)} = 5$ (a Triplet)

Right-angled triangles are therefore either made of Pythagorean Triplets or generate irrational numbers. This is why such 'irrational numbers' were very precious, so the ancient Egyptians devised a geometric way to generate them using 'root rectangles.'

Constructing the root rectangles

We start with the most basic of figures, a square with all sides equal to 1 unit. It does not matter if the sides are one inch, one cubit, one meter or even one mile.

1. Draw a diagonal between opposite corners, forming two right-angled triangles. Then, using Pythagoras' Theorem, we can work out the length of the sides of this triangle and in so doing generate our first irrational length:

hypotenuse² = side 1² + side 2²
hypotenuse² = 1² + 1²
hypotenuse² = 1 + 1 = 2
Therefore, the hypotenuse = √2

$$\text{hypotenuse}^2 = \text{side } 1^2 + \text{side } 2^2$$
$$\text{hypotenuse}^2 = 1^2 + 1^2$$
$$\text{hypotenuse}^2 = 1 + 1 = 2$$
$$\text{Therefore, the hypotenuse} = \sqrt{2}$$

2. Now place a compass point at the end of the diagonal and set it to the length of the diagonal. Then draw an arc.

3. Extend the square's side to create a new rectangle (the red triangle in the diagram above). Draw its diagonal—this will be exactly √3 long. Thus we have generated our second irrational number.

4. Repeat the process as often as you like, each time creating a new diagonal. This produces √4, or double square, √5 and so on. Of course, the √4 is not irrational at all, but equal to 2, forming a double square.

This is how our ancestors measured and generated these irrational numbers. As you can see these numbers are 'irrational' only if you insist upon using the decimal system. Geometrically, they are much more straightforward, being basically the diagonals of simply constructed rectangles.

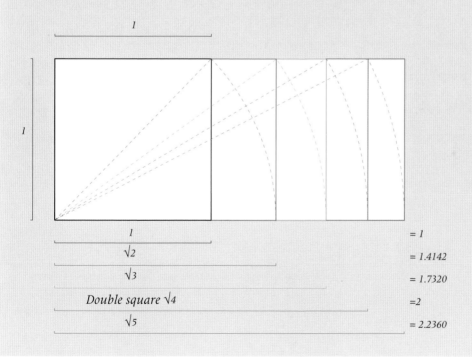

1
1
1

1 = *1*
√2 = *1.4142*
√3 = *1.7320*
Double square √4 = 2
√5 = *2.2360*

LEFT Starting with a square (of side 1 unit) and using simply a compass and rules, you can construct root rectangles of lengths √2, √3 and √5.

The five Platonic solids

Regular polygons are multisided figures than can be inscribed within a circle so that all their vertices (corners) touch that circle. Likewise, regular solid polygons may be inscribed within a sphere, with all vertices touching its surface. Their faces are made up of regular polygons.

Plato called these 3-D polygons perfect, and he defined five solids:

Tetrahedron	4-sided
	(tetra = 4)
Hexahedron/cube	6-sided
	(hexa = 6)
Octahedron	8-sided
	(octa = 8)
Dodecahedron	12-sided
	(dodeca = 12)
Icosahedron	20-sided
	(icosa = 20)

These five solids became an important part of both practical and mystical geometry, although Plato was not the first to think of them: the first three belong to Pythagoras and the last two to Theaetetus (in the fourth century BC).

Millions of shapes are composed of *irregular* polygons, but only five solids can be made up of *regular* polygons. Because of this rarity, Aristotle and Plato assumed they formed the building blocks of matter and so matched the five solids with the four classical elements plus ether.

Hedron simply means surface, so the regular *polyhedrons* are 3-D shapes made up of surfaces that are symmetrical multisided figures (see table below).

You can relate all these multisided figures together using the very useful master formula:

Number of edges + 2 = number of faces + number of vertices

Although the solids look complex they are actually quite simple:

THE FIVE PLATONIC SOLIDS IN DETAIL

Element	Platonic solids	Number of edges	Number of planes	Number of faces	Number of vertices (corners)	Shape of the face
Ether	Dodecahedron	30	60	12	20	Pentagon
Fire	Tetrahedron	6	12	4	4	Triangle
Air	Octahedron	12	24	8	6	Triangle
Water	Icosahedron	30	60	20	12	Triangle
Earth	Hexahedron (cube)	12	24	6	8	Square

Tetrahedron/pyramid

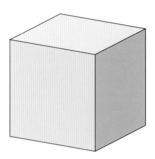

Hexahedron/cube

Octahedron

• The cube is the most basic regular box shape.

• The tetrahedron is a pyramid with a triangular base.

• The octahedron is two identical, square-based pyramids joined together.

The five solids form two pairs of elements, duals, plus ether. The cube (earth) and the octahedron (air) are geometric 'duals,' meaning that one can be created inside the other by connecting the midpoints of all the faces. So you can generate a cube inside an octahedron, inside a cube, inside an octahedron and so on, forever.

Likewise the other two elements represented by the tetrahedron (fire) and the icosahedron (water) are duals and can generate each other.

So there is perfect symmetry between the two pairs of elements, earth–air and fire–water. The dodecahedron is a dual to itself, therefore ether can generate itself.

LEFT The five Platonic solids were associated with the four ancient elements and ether (the upper air) and are the only perfectly pure regular solids.

Dodecahedron

Icosahedron

The 13 Archimedean solids

The five Platonic solids are 'pure' and contain only one type of polygon.
Archimedes (c.287–212 BC) described 13 additional solids that contain two
or more different types of polygons.

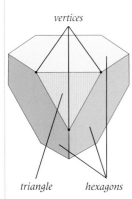

vertices

triangle   hexagons

ABOVE The composition of a truncated tetrahedron, which is made up of regular hexagonal and triangular faces meeting at 12 vertices.

Archimedes' original writings on the topic have been lost. During the Renaissance all but one of the solids were gradually rediscovered, until Johannes Kepler (1571–1630), in his quest to find the solution to the sacred numbers behind the planetary orbits (see pages 78–79) finally reconstructed the entire set.

Each face of the 13 Archimedean solids is a symmetrical, regular polygon. The polygons are all built from the basic Euclidean building blocks. Around every vertex (corner) of a solid, the same polygons always appear in exactly the same sequence. For example, in the truncated tetrahedron, each vertex 'hosts' a hexagon–triangle–hexagon sequence.

To properly appreciate these solids you need to look at the relationship between the numbers of vertices, edges and faces (see table below). The faces are divided up according to how many sides each face has. When they are sorted according to their vertices, a clear pattern emerges. With only one exception, the icosidodecahedron, the vertices are all multiples of 12.

The 13 solids are described by listing the types of polygons that are hosted by each vertex—this is enough to identify each one. Each of the 24 vertices of the truncated hexahedron (or truncated cube) for example, hosts a sequence of a triangle (three sides), an octagon (eight sides) and another octagon (eight sides)—so it can simply be referred to as a 3, 8, 8. It is important, however, to note the order of the numbers describing the polyhedrons, especially when the number of faces meeting at a vertex exceeds three.

THE 13 ARCHIMEDEAN SOLIDS IN DETAIL

Archimedean Solid	Vertices	Edges	Total faces	Triangular faces (3)	Square faces (4)	Pentagonal faces (5)	Hexagonal faces (6)	Octagonal) faces (8	Decagonal faces (10)
Truncated tetrahedron	12	18	8		4			4	
Cuboctahedron	12	24	14	8	6				
Truncated cube	24	36	14	8				6	
Truncated octahedron	24	36	14		6		8		
Small rhombicuboctahedron	24	48	6		8	18			
Snub cube	24	6	38	32	6				
Icosidodecahedron	30	60	32	20		12			
Great rhombicuboctahedron	48	72	26		12		8	6	
Truncated dodecahedron	60	90	32	20					12
Truncated icosahedron	60	90	32			12	20		
Small rhombicosidodecahedron	60	120	62	20	30	12			
Snub dodecahedron	60	150	92	80		12			
Great rhombicosidodecahedron	120	80	62		30		20		12

PLATONIC SOLIDS

Tetrahedron/pyramid

Hexahedron/cube

Octahedron

Dodecahedron

Icosahedron

ARCHIMEDEAN SOLIDS

Truncated tetrahedron

Truncated cube

Cuboctahedron

Small rhombi-cuboctahedron

Great rhombicubocta-hedron

Snub cube

Truncated octahedron

Truncated dodecahedron

Icosidodecahedron

Small rhombico-sidodecahedron

Great rhombico-sidodecahedron

Snub dodecahedron

Truncated icosahedron

How are they constructed?

Seven of the 13 Archimedean solids can be obtained by truncating one of the Platonic solids. Truncation is the process of cutting off the corners of an existing solid, resulting in a new face for each previously existing vertex. For example, it replaces the square face (four edges) with an octagonal face (eight edges), giving octagons instead of squares.

Two of the Archimedean solids (the small rhombicosidodecahedron and rhombicuboctahedron) can be obtained by the opposite process, the expansion of a Platonic solid, so in a way they are all derived from the basic five Platonic solids.

The remaining two solids, the snub cube and snub dodecahedron, can be obtained by moving the faces of a cube and dodecahedron outward while giving each face a twist.

Snub is a process of surrounding each polygon with a border of triangles—for example, deriving the snub cube from the cube. The resulting spaces are then filled with a chain of equilateral triangles.

ABOVE The 13 Archimedean solids are made up of a mixture of regular faces, such as triangles, squares, pentagons and octagons.

The world of fractals

Fractals belong to a non-Euclidean way of looking at the universe. They are geometric shapes or patterns that help to describe the forces of growth and are therefore a part of sacred geometry. Fractals now have applications in astronomy, economics, meteorology and also in special effects used in cinematography.

In 1975 the French mathematician Benoit Mandelbrot defined fractals as objects that do not lose their detail or their proportions when they are magnified or shrunk, even to the microscopic level. This property is highly reminiscent of *phi* (the Golden Mean, or 1.618), where the same essential and sacred proportion is retained every time you cut the line or the rectangle (see pages 34–39). In fact, the qualities of both fractals and phi are concerned with growth.

Features of fractals

There are two different types of fractal, the geometric fractal and the random fractal. The snowflake is an example of a geometric fractal that grows (in the simplest terms) by the addition of equilateral triangles in specific patterns.

Random fractals are computer generated, in both modelling and games.

Fractal geometry can lead to convincing images of natural growth phenomena, such as coastlines, ferns and tree bark. They can also emerge from climate and even apparently manmade phenomena, such as stock price graphs or economic predictions, which show self-similarity.

Some ferns are classic natural examples of a fractal, with each section (pinna) of leaf being a miniature replication of the whole leaf. A single pinna if magnified looks like a whole leaf. In addition, in some species, their buds unfold in the shape of a logarithmic spiral. This means that nature does not have to redesign the leaf at every stage of its growth, but the initial design just keeps on replicating.

One thing that is sometimes overlooked is that natural fractals, as distinct from theoretical and mathematically generated ones, do have an end. The fractal that describes the map of the coast of the Britain can be examined under greater and greater magnification until you reach, say, the configuration of the grains of sand on a beach. You cannot go into a finer molecular degree of detail and expect the pattern to repeat, as you could with a purely mathematical fractal.

The other important feature of fractals is scaling. In a fractal the degree of

RIGHT **Each bract on the cone of the pinus nigra pine cone lies on the intersection of two spirals that wind in opposite directions around the cone from pole to pole.**

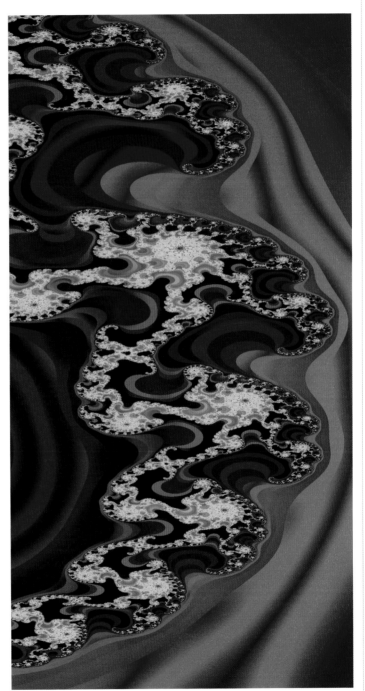

ABOVE The coastlines of Scotland and Ireland will retain their fractal nature as you get closer and closer to them.

RIGHT Beautifully curving lines with endless self-similarity at any scale are generated by the Mandelbrot set.

irregularity or fragmentation is identical at all scales. Fractals do not get smoother as the magnification brings you closer; they simply continue to generate new irregularities that are commensurate with the speed at which you zoom in on them.

Order not chaos

Fractals are popularly supposed to be associated with the mathematics of chaos, but they are, in fact, very ordered—just millions of interlocking, self-replicating, natural objects. They only look chaotic yet are governed by a definite geometry. A case in point is the movement of clouds, which are definitely fractal in nature: their outline looks chaotic but is actually a fractal controlled by the inherent properties of the interaction of water vapor with air and dust particles. The essence of measuring or describing a fractal is to isolate the basic pattern—what is called its initial recursive mathematical function. Interestingly, the Fibonacci series is one such recursive function.

PART 2

THE GEOMETRY OF NATURE

The numbers venerated by Pythagoras and the geometry enunciated by Euclid are reflected in nature. Documenting the mathematics of the growth of living creatures is difficult, but it can be seen in the forms of shells or horns— the concrete traces of growth. In the nautilus and in fossil ammonites we can clearly see the geometry of successive chambers adhering very closely to the geometry of the logarithmic spiral. In the horns of animals we can see similar spirals governed by other geometric formulae.

In plant life the easiest numbers to measure are those of seeds in a flower or the angles at which successive leaves or branches grow from a central stem. Both these occurences are found to follow the Fibonacci series, and there are fixed angles of generation.

In the mineral world the huge array of crystals utilizes only seven different geometric forms. The structure, properties and qualities of that universal solvent and support of life, water, in both its liquid and snow forms, subscribe to the same geometry. Finally, at the molecular level lies the subtle geometry of DNA—a double helix surrounding a double pentagonal structure. Truly, the geometry of nature is sacred.

LEFT Like water, air adopts a spiral form in tornadoes or storms, which shows up clearly on satellite pictures.

CHAPTER 3

LIFE'S GEOMETRY

Because geometry forms the ground plan behind the physical universe, we might expect to find it also in the design of both animate and inanimate natural things. This chapter looks at the geometry found in nature, especially in patterns of growth, and relates it to the curves and spirals discussed in Part 1. The emphasis is on a pattern that is either repeatable or can be duplicated. For all nature's apparent richness, the pattern is, like the fractal, amazingly complex but based on very simple building blocks.

At the 'hard end' of the scale we have the structure of crystals, which are formed under intense temperature and pressure according to just seven simple types of geometric shape. Each mineral usually follows one of these patterns. The mineralized shell of some animals, such as the nautilus bivalve, extend themselves using the geometry of the logarithmic spiral, as do the horns of some sheep. Plants also use replication of different numerical scales as their means of growth. Even water responds to geometric forms in its helical flow along a riverbed or the structure of its form as snowflakes, which can be described in terms of fractals.

Plant growth geometry

The growth of living things consists of replicating patterns. A plant produces leaves that conform to the pattern inherent in its species—they grow out from a stem at geometrically predictable intervals.

ABOVE **The unfurling fronds of a fern adhere to a strict geometric form.**

In 1753 the Scottish botanist Robert Simson realized that Fibonacci's series (see pages 38–39) governed the growth pattern of many plants. Essentially it maps the geometry of growth—the equiangular spiral and *phi* (Golden Mean, see pages 34–39) are found in the spacing of leaves on a stem, in petal numbers and in the arrangement of seedheads.

Leaf spacing

Look down on a straight plant stem from above and you will see that the leaves protrude from the stem in a spiral pattern. This gives each leaf (or branch) access to the maximum amount of sun or rain.

By tracing your finger from leaf to leaf around the stem you can establish the order of growth—it takes the shape of a helix. You can also establish two numbers: the total number of leaves protruding from the stem and the number of times (rotations) your finger moved around the stem in order to count the leaves.

The following formula determines the plant 'growth spiral angle', which is the number of degrees between each leaf protrusion: Plant growth spiral angle = number of rotations x 360/number of leaves produced.

This calculation often comes out to exactly 137 degrees, 30 minutes and 27 seconds, which equals $360/phi^2$. The angle is sometimes called the Golden Angle.

One result of the plant using this angle is that the leaves that protrude directly above the first one are leaves 5, 8, 13, 21, 34 … It's that familiar sequence again. In true Fibonacci form, the alignment is not perfect (out by 0.06, 0.03, 0.02, 0.01 …) but gradually converges on perfection.

Arrangement of seedheads

The clearest visual examples of the presence of Fibonacci's numbers are sunflowers and pine cones. The sunflower seedhead consists of two interlocking spirals—one left-handed and one right-handed. There may be eight right-handed spirals and 13 left-handed spirals, each seed belonging to both. Other pairs include 34 and 55, or 55 and 89.

Petal numbers

The Fibonacci series also seems to determine how many petals a plant will have on its flowers:

3	Lilies, irises, triliums
5	Columbines, primroses, buttercups, wild roses, larkspurs
8	Delphiniums, sanguinarias, cosmos
13	Cineraria, corn marigold
21	Chicory, Black-eyed Susan
34	Plantain, pyrethrum
55	Aster novi-belgii
89	Michaelmas daisies

The number of petals never reaches 144—a number that is often found to be limiting in other examples of the Fibonacci series in nature.

Crystal structure

The hermetic axiom 'as above, so below' can be extended to read 'as in the atoms so in the outer structure,' at least in the case of crystalline minerals. Under ideal conditions, crystals form perfect structures that reflect the arrangement of their atoms. Geologists group crystals into seven orders according to their geometry.

In 1912 the German physicist Max von Laue passed X-rays through a crystal ball on to an unexposed photographic plate. When the plate was developed he saw dark points arranged in perfect symmetry. His technique of X-ray crystallography enabled scientists to work out the geometric structure of crystals of various minerals. At the same time, the vibration of crystals was used for receiving radio waves—in old-fashioned crystal radio sets a polyhedron crystal created, or responded to, a particular frequency.

It is also because of the energy of this inherent structure that they form into beautiful shapes. Their creation under extremes of temperature and pressure in the bowels of the Earth allows the

configuration of their constituent atoms to control the outcome in terms of crystalline geometric form. Simple whole numbers govern the electron shells of the atoms (see page 21) and the resulting configurations of crystals.

Crystals naturally grow in the shape of polyhedra—that is, as solid shapes whose faces are polygons. They are the closest physical representations of Plato's solids, although not as perfectly formed as his ideal forms (see pages 54–55). Crystals of a specific substance will always adopt the same shape: they can be formed of regular or irregular polyhedra, but not both. The simplest example is probably ordinary table salt (sodium chloride), which, if mixed in a very concentrated solution with hot water, will crystallize out in a series of six-sided, cube-like crystals on cooling. A chrome alum solution, on the other hand, naturally forms octahedral (eight-sided) crystals.

Crystals build up in a similar manner to the growth of living forms: the process of crystallization consists of the creation of tiny duplicates of the original form, which are then 'stacked' together to form a much larger version of exactly the same shape. Of course, in nature perfect forms are rare, and the end result is often affected by being jostled by adjacent structures during growth.

RIGHT **Halite crystals follow a cubic crystal formation, with a second similar formulation impinging at an angle.**

Ordering crystals

There are seven orders of crystals, each distinguished from the next by just one change in the structure. Analyzing a particular crystal's geometry, and measuring the angle between its planes as well as the relationship of one axis to another, will determine the group to which it belongs.

Cubic crystals These are the most basic crystals—an example is ordinary table salt. To put it more technically, they have three mutually perpendicular axes of equal length that produce six faces, and form that archetypal three-dimensional object, the cube. Each face is a square. Examples include iron pyrites, alum, garnet and galena. The Cube of Space is the image used by the earliest Kabbalistic text, the *Sepher Yetzirah*, to describe the initial structure of the whole of creation. It has six directions and can be visualized as a basic cubic crystal.

Tetragonal crystals Only two of the three axes are the same length, but they are all perpendicular. These crystals have rectangular faces. Examples include cassiterite and rutile.

Orthorhombic crystals All three axes are of different lengths, but they are all perpendicular. Examples include topaz, chrysoberyl, peridot and chalcotite.

Monoclinic crystals All three axes are of different lengths and only two are perpendicular. Examples include borax, azurite and muscovite.

Triclinic crystals All three axes are of different lengths and not one is perpendicular to any other. These are not common.

Rhombohedral or trigonal crystals All three axes are of equal length, but not one is perpendicular to any other.

Hexagonal crystals These are the most complex. They have four axes, three of which are of equal length and lie on the same plane with an angle of 120 degrees (the angle of junction) between them. The fourth axis is perpendicular to the three and can be of any length. Examples include calcite, tourmaline and beryl.

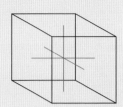
Cubic crystal

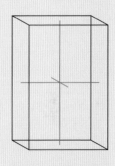
Orthorhombic crystal

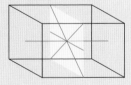
Rhombohedral or trigonal crystal

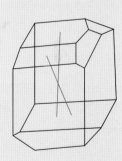
Triclinic crystal

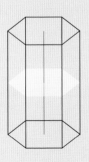
Hexagonal crystal

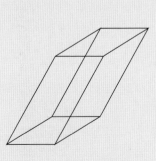
Monoclinic crystal

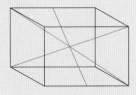
Tetragonal crystal

Living spirals

Geometry governs the growth of many creatures, especially in the sea, where pentagonal shapes are very common. The logarithmic spiral is also instrumental in the growth of other living things (such as the fetal development of many animals), but it is most obvious where a concrete form like a shell is left behind. The spiral whorls of many seashells or the Dall sheep's horns are a case in point.

The geometry of the spiral manifests in nature as a form of proportional growth. The most often quoted examples are the living nautilus and the fossil ammonite. Both are or were soft-bodied creatures constricted inside rigid shells. Unable to grow bigger like mammals, they constantly build new and larger shell chambers around themselves, rather than, say, expanding in a straight line.

BELOW A beautiful nautilus shell showing its successively developed chambers, each larger than but as perfectly proportioned as the previous one.

The nautilus

As it moves into its new and larger chamber, the nautilus fills the old chamber with gas and closes it off with a perfect layer of nacre (mother of pearl). It occupies only the outermost chamber, but leaves a tiny thread, or tail, that winds back to its tiny original chamber. Each additional chamber is exactly proportional to the previous smaller chambers—a feat of biological engineering that uses the logarithmic spiral (see pages 48–51), a geometric shape that retains a constant angle with respect to its original center. This allows maximum room for additional growth for the minimum of labor—it is obviously a winning formula, as the nautilus species has been around for millions of years.

Art imitates nature, and Leonardo da Vinci's bust of Scipio Africanus features a helmet whose main ornamentation is a shell cast in a classic spiral form.

Horns with spirals

The horn is another form of organic structure that preserves its pattern of growth in a rigid form as it grows. The spiral extensions of the horns of the Dall sheep and other antelope incorporate the logarithmic spiral found in the nautilus.

While the nautilus utilizes a flat spiral, forms such as the horns of the greater kudu of Central Africa grow in a 3-D spiral. This is a spiral that has grown around a cone or similar geometric form and tapers to a point.

Apart from being symptomatic of growth by replication, the spiral also has the shock-absorbing properties of a spring, which would be of advantage in the design of horns meant for the clash of battle. Interestingly, the domesticated varieties of horned animals show a completely different geometric twist structure from their wild cousins. This structure is based on the direction of twist, and the horns are called homonymous. These horns exhibit a right-hand spiral twist in the horn on the right side of the animal's head and a left-turning spiral of the horn on the left side of the animal's head. This homonymous formation is found in the horns of all domesticated animals but not in any wild animals of the same or similar species.

The spiral appears in the shape of horns (above), the fossilized chambers of an ammonite (right) and the floating structure of a colony of salps (below).

Other animals

The geometry inherent in animal life is also exhibited by the patterns spiders use when spinning their webs. These patterns follow a number of mathematical models, including logarithmic spirals. The shape of an egg, designed to easily be laid, without breaking, is an example of ovoid geometry in life. Other natural occurences said to utilize this geometry include the wings of butterflies and the calico surfperch also conforms to these spirals. Even at the microscopic level, spiral forms of protozoa have been discovered. Bees construct the cells of their hive using the hexagon as their model.

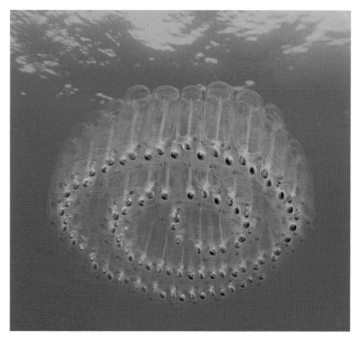

Living water

We have seen that the growth patterns and structure of mineral crystals, plants and animals are governed by simple geometry. It is perhaps hard to believe that anything that is as simple or as fluid as water can be conditioned by geometry—but it is!

Water is, of course, anything but pure and simple. It is an almost universal solvent and makes up more than 60 percent of our bodies. We wouldn't last a week without it. A drop in temperature of a few degrees from 4°C (39°F) to just below 0°C (32°F), when energy is actually removed from it, turns water from a totally pliable liquid into a solid that is capable of breaking metal pipes.

Victor Schauberger's discoveries

One of the unsung heroes of 20th-century science, Victor Schauberger (1885–1958) realized that at 4°C (39°F) water is at its

BELOW Water flowing down a geometrically designed flowform, which improves its quality and oxygen content.

densest and can float materials that it could not ordinarily support. So, in his native Austria, Schauberger built temperature-controlled flumes (water shutes or slides) to carry larger pieces of timber much longer distances than could normally be expected. In fact, slight changes in the geometry of a river could make the water deposit silt or, conversely, scour and deepen the riverbed. Schauberger devised a means of embedding geometrically curved blades in the bed of a river to drive the water into a helical spin. The results were remarkable and life-giving: his methods cleared previously stagnant pools, leading to a measurable increase in the amount of oxygen the water absorbed and leading to a rapid rise in the concentration of fish life.

After the Second World War Schauberger developed vortex action (rather than the usual turbine design) as a means of generating power from water. In 1958, promises of funding attracted him to the United States, but he ended up losing his writings, prototypes and rights. Five days after returning home to Austria he died.

His son founded the Pythagoras–Kepler System Institute in Lauffen, near Salzburg, which still exists today. It is very revealing that the names chosen for his institute were two of the key names in the history of sacred geometry.

The geometry of meandering

The natural geometry of a river (particularly on a gentle incline) is the side-to-side meander, with a regular mathematical alternation of shallows and deep pools, if the quality of the underlying sediment is the same. As part of this geometry, the river generates currents, which also alternate between scouring deep pools at bends and depositing the scoured material on the opposite bank further downstream. The whole shape of the meander consequently moves sideways, like a giant sine wave, slowly downstream.

Man's misguided attempts to straighten meandering river flows, or fix them with stone and concrete banks, has inflicted real damage. The geometry of meandering is adapted to cope with differing volumes, according to the level of rainfall in the headwaters of the rivers. Artificially straightening the channels alters the speed of flow and causes more frequent and more extreme floods to occur.

Water flowforms

Many of Schauberger's advanced ideas have still not been fully utilized. One experimenter who has taken Schauberger's theories a step further is Englishman John Wilkes, who has invented a type of water flow that spins water from side to side, or in a figure of eight, as it descends a series of specially designed pottery or concrete 'flowforms'. These bowls or dishes mimic the shape of the flow that is created when one stream of water pours into another—a sort of natural 'wake' similar to the ones that fascinated Leonardo da Vinci.

These flowforms stimulate a more extreme version of the movements that a healthy river would make and, according, to its inventor, measurably improves the quality of the water so treated. So here we have a delightful combination of aesthetics, geometrical design and a real change in the quality of the water brought about by that geometry.

BELOW **A meandering river on a mature floodplain never runs straight but forms meanders, which are a precise geometric response to volume and silt load.**

Spiralling flows

A special form of the helix, the spiral, is intimately linked with the movements of water, as shown in whirlpools or, on a smaller scale, in your bath as the bath water disappears down the plughole. Air, like water, is a fluid, and so tornados, hurricanes and whirlwinds also adopt the same geometry.

Snowflake wonderland

ABOVE Even though there are many hexagonal forms, each arm of the same snowflake is symmetrical with its other arms.

The structure of a snowflake is one of the clearest manifestations of fractals in nature. This may be because it forms when water falls freely through the atmosphere without interference from adjacent objects. No other substance crystallizes in so many different ways.

Despite such variety, the geometry that governs the growth of one of a snowflake's branches will also govern the growth of its other branches. It is almost as if some strange geometric coordination is happening. No matter what scale is used to view the final product, the pattern is seen to be the same. However, such figures do not have the smoothness of Euclidean geometry, where everything is either a straight line, a circle or a smooth curve that can be generated by slicing through a cone (the so-called conic sections).

The structure of snowflakes

The procedure of generating the Koch fractal representation of a snowflake described on page 71 may not reflect what

BELOW Snowflakes build into many thousands of different designs, all based on hexagonal geometry. This enables even heavy snowfalls to lie on steep inclines.

actually happens structurally on a freezing cold day, but it gives a fair mathematical representation of the fractal nature of a snowflake. It also demonstrates that, given a sharp enough pencil and superhuman eyesight, the process could go on till you reach the infinitesimally small.

With fractal geometry (see pages 58–59) the length of the perimeter of the figure continually increases without limit, but the area will expand only very slowly. The length of the perimeter of the snowflake depends on the degree of magnification that is used.

In fact, it can be shown mathematically that the area of the snowflake will never exceed ⅗ or 1.6 times the area of the original generating triangle. There are those Fibonacci numbers again!

Effectively, the area of the snowflake is finite while the perimeter is (potentially, as least) infinite—this is a characteristic of all fractal geometric objects. Of course, in the real world, there must be some kind of limit, and with the snowflake it is at the molecular level.

The reason why the Koch figure starts as a hexagram is because in nature the geometry of snowflake bonds is bound up with the angle of 60 degrees. We know there are very few shapes that will neatly cluster around a point. One such shape is formed of six equilateral triangles whose angles are 60 degrees. As 6 x 60 = 360, the resulting structure will be hexagonal.

The number six

The Chinese also had a numerical explanation for the qualities of the snowflake. Perhaps the earliest reference was in 135 BC when Han Ying wrote: "Flowers of plants and trees are generally five-pointed, but those of snow … are always six-pointed." The scholar T'ang Chin was reasoning like a Pythagorean when he explained that "since six is the true number of water, when water congeals into flowers (snowflakes) they must be six-pointed."

Centuries later, it was Johannes Kepler who in 1611 asked "why always six-sided?" and attempted to work out the geometry. It was not until the English polymath Robert Hooke (1635–1703) looked at them through a microscope in the 1600s—and then made sketches— that their form was fully appreciated in the West. Hooke also contributed to our understanding of the harmonic motion of springs, and anticipated several of Newton's discoveries.

Freezing water

An interesting light is thrown on the geometry of the formation of ice crystals by the strange behavior of freezing water. Water reaches its maximum density at just below 4°C (39°F). Below this temperature water actually becomes less dense as it freezes, and so ice floats. The hexagonal form of snowflakes reasserts itself in ice, as each water molecule is hydrogen-bonded in an arrangement that displays hexagonal symmetry. It therefore seems likely that the structure of snow-flakes is affected by molecular bonding, or, as the ancient Chinese scientist has it, "Six is the true number of water."

The Koch snowflake

In 1904 the mathematician Helge von Koch (1870–1924) devised a mathematical model that produces just one snowflake design. It begins with a single equilateral triangle. To generate this snowflake curve:

1. Begin with an equilateral triangle.

2. Superimpose a second reversed equilateral triangle on it to form a hexagram.

3. Take each triangular vertex and convert it into an equilateral triangle pointing outwards, then draw the reverse equilateral triangle over it.

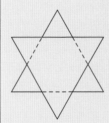

4. Delete that part of this hexagram that lies in the old triangle.

5. Continue this process with each point of the initial hexagram.

6. Repeat, fractally, at finer and finer levels of detail.

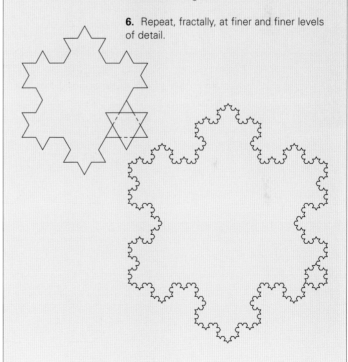

The geometry of genetics

The helix is a 3-D spiral that is closely related to growth. Common examples in the living world are seen in the growth of climbers, especially honeysuckle, morning glory and bindweed, and in the horns of antelopes, rams and narwhals. The spiral staircase, twisted steel cable, wood screws, telephone cables, springs and the corkscrew are all manmade helices.

ABOVE The caduceus wand was the symbol of Hermes, the messenger of the gods in Greek mythology.

Helices can spiral clockwise or anti-clockwise (counter-clockwise) and are therefore referred to as right-handed or left-handed respectively—one is the mirror reflection of the other. The helix also occurs in weather, in storms, cyclones and hurricanes.

The double helix is an even more interesting shape. Long before the discovery of DNA, the standard symbol for medicine was a double helix of two serpents coiled around a wand. This is actually the caduceus or magic wand of the Greek god Hermes (Roman equivalent of Mercury), messenger of the gods, purveyor of (magical) incantations, conductor of the dead and protector of merchants, tricksters and thieves. Alchemists were referred to as the 'sons of Hermes' and as practitioners of the hermetic arts. There are clear occult associations with the caduceus, too.

BELOW The perfect spiral or helix governs the structure of this shell.

The double helix of DNA

Deoxyribonucleic acid, or DNA for short, is composed of two right-handed 3-D helices. In 1953 Dr James Watson and Dr Francis Crick discovered the structure of this double helix and, with Dr Maurice Wilkins, received the 1962 Nobel Prize for 'their discoveries of the molecular structure of nucleic acids and its significance for information transfer in living material.' By 'information transfer' they meant genetic inheritance.

DNA combines into strands called chromosomes. Different species have a different number of chromosomes: humans have 46 (23 pairs). One curious coincidence is that if you use Greek isopsephy to add the value of the letters in Adam, our biblical genetic ancestor, they come to 46.

DNA is like a spiral ladder with a series of rungs holding together the two strands.

The DNA double helix requires ten rungs to make a complete turn—the Kabbalistic Tree of Life also has a ladder of ten rungs, and ten was Pythagoras' number of completion.

Every living cell is made of just six elements—carbon, hydrogen, oxygen, phosphorus, nitrogen, and sulphur, which have almost adjacent atomic numbers 1, 5, 6, 7, 15, and 16. Together they weave one of the most complex and self-replicating patterns.

The rungs of the DNA ladder are composed of molecules called nucleotides, of which there are four types. Each type is linked to one of the strands with a sugar phosphate molecule. The details of the structure are complicated, yet the system has a simple modular pattern. In fact, modern gene research regularly engineers this structure and can modify or replace modules at will in the laboratory. Like the logarithmic spiral, the geometry can be easily replicated (but better packed), and its facility for self-replication and growth is built into the geometry of the DNA molecule.

Double pentagons

The geometry that governs this spiral can best be seen if you look vertically down the spiral, as it were. What you will see is a structure that is reminiscent of *phi*, Φ (the Golden Mean): a series of double pentagons that make up the composite axial view of the DNA double helix. Each full rotation of the double-helical coil contains ten sugar phosphate molecules.

Phi is closely associated with 'fiveness' and is integral to the construction of the pentagon (see page 36). It turns up frequently in the structure of component

pentagons and again in the relationship between the pentagons. The simplest geometric pattern of the DNA axial view reveals three major double pentagons. Each pentagon intersects with two other pentagons. In other words, these intersections are loaded with the Golden Mean buried in the axial structure of that singular molecule, the DNA double helix.

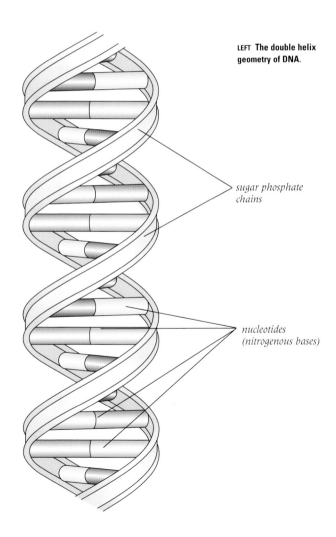

LEFT The double helix geometry of DNA.

sugar phosphate chains

nucleotides (nitrogenous bases)

CHAPTER 4

GEOMETRY IN ASTRONOMY AND COSMOLOGY

The expression 'harmony of the spheres' sums up the early conviction that there are strict mathematical and geometric relationships between the orbits of the planets—this was later proved to be correct by Kepler. Even if early astronomers, such as Ptolemy, were wrong about the central position of the Earth, they still generated geometric models of great complexity that did explain the apparently eccentric movement of the planets. Johannes Kepler even utilized the geometry of the five Platonic solids in his early attempts to establish the geometry of planetary orbits around a new center, the Sun.

The Ancients measured the positions and movements of the stars by their rising and setting points, as marked on the horizon. These points— particularly for the Sun and Moon— became important in the construction of the megalithic monuments, whose alignments on Earth reflected the alignments in the heavens.

The geometry of the heavens is also reflected in the geographic geometry of the Earth. Attempts to map both the heavens and the Earth made it necessary to define a starting point meridian for the lines of longitude. Even if now Greenwich is universally accepted as this line, as late as the early 20th century the Paris meridian held considerable sway.

The night sky

The Ancients understood the celestial mechanics behind the nightly display of stars and planets, and they applied this knowledge to the sacred geometry they used in the construction of their temples.

ABOVE **Johannes Kepler marks the turning point between heliocentric and earth-centerd astronomy.**

As the Earth orbits around the Sun it rotates on its axis, which is tilted at 23.5 degrees to the plane of that orbit. This axis of rotation always points to the same star, the Pole Star, no matter where the Earth is in its progression around the Sun. The Ancients, especially the Chinese, thought that the Pole Star was a very important part of the machinery of the universe, perhaps more important than the Sun, although nowadays most urban dwellers would be hard pressed even to identify it.

The fixed stars

Imagine lying on your back on soft grass and watching the sphere of the fixed stars 'wheel' overhead. In fact, they only appear to rotate around the Earth: it is the Earth's rotation that makes them appear to move. Of the many star groups, or constellations, the Ancients chose 12 to be special markers, and these became the 12 signs of the Zodiac.

The Zodiac is the band of stars that stretches 8 degrees either side of the Sun's apparent path through the sky. This path is called the ecliptic, and the Zodiac is wide enough to also accommodate the paths of the Sun, the Moon and all the planets. It is therefore a key part of the geometry of the heavens.

In the Northern Hemisphere, the Pole Star—also known as Polaris (see pages 80–81)—always stays in the same place in the sky. All the other stars seem to 'move' in circular paths around Polaris, once every 24 hours. Most of these will appear to rise over the eastern horizon and set at the western horizon, except for the stars very close to the Pole Star. The stars close to the Pole Star will inscribe a circle around it, without disappearing beneath the horizon at any time. The Ancients portrayed the stars as fixed to the inside surface of a large sphere, which turned around the Earth and pivoted on the Pole Star. This is a much clearer image than any modern description.

Of course, we see the stars move around only part of their circular path because during the day sunlight drowns out starlight. Moreover, the part of the total starry vault we can see depends on which hemisphere we are in.

Anyone who has lain on their back at night and watched the stars will know that the stars are fixed in only one sense— in relation to one another. The whole net of fixed stars circle together, rising up from one horizon across the night sky, then disappearing beneath the Earth's rim at the other horizon. It is not just the Sun that rises and sets.

The Sun

Modern man, if asked, will say without thinking that the Sun rises in the east and sets in the west. In fact, this happens only on precisely two days of the year. The rest of the time, the rising position of the sun appears to migrate along the eastern horizon. In the Northern Hemisphere this

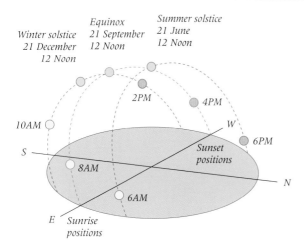

Winter solstice
21 December
12 Noon

Equinox
21 September
12 Noon

Summer solstice
21 June
12 Noon

2PM

4PM

10AM

W

6PM

S

Sunset
positions

8AM

N

6AM

E Sunrise
positions

ABOVE LEFT **The path of the sun at different times of the year, showing that it rises and sets at different points on the horizon during the course of the year.**

ABOVE RIGHT **The night sky with a full Moon rising above the horizon.**

rising point travels from the southeast (in winter) to the northeast (in summer), and the reverse in the Southern Hemisphere. Likewise, the setting position of the Sun appears to migrate along the horizon from the southwest (in the Northern Hemisphere winter) to the northwest (in summer).

The Sun reaches its most northerly point (appearing closest to Polaris) on about 21 June in the Northern Hemisphere, when it is in the Zodiacal sign of Cancer: at noon on that day it is directly overhead on the Tropic of Cancer, at precisely 23.5 degrees north of the Equator. This is the piece of information that Eratosthenes used to measure the circumference of the Earth (see pages 26–27). This fact will also become important when we look at the geometry of Stonehenge (see pages 110–111), which is oriented to the rising point of the sun at midsummer.

The changing daily path of the Sun's course causes the seasons—warmer and therefore summer when it moves further north, cooler and therefore winter when it retreats to the south. The opposite seasons occur in the Southern Hemisphere— summer when the Sun moves south, winter when it moves north.

The Moon

The Ancients also knew that the Moon orbits the Earth once every 29.531 days, with the plane of its orbit tilted at 5 degrees to the plane of the Earth's orbit around the Sun. The Moon appears to follow a much more complicated dance than the Sun because it also revolves round the Earth, yet it still rises and sets. Its movements have long been important in measuring the passage of time (see pages 84–85).

The cycles of the Moon also affect the tides (important for fisherman and sailors), sowing (important for farmers), magic (important for magicians and priests) and menstrual cycles (important for women and, therefore, for everyone).

Sighting points

Fixing a point on a moving target (the fixed stars) in the middle of the sky was difficult without precision sighting tubes that had adequate calibration. So the Babylonians and Egyptians figured that it was much simpler to map the point and the time when a particular heavenly body rose above the eastern horizon or set below the western horizon. These sighting points formed the basis of the whole of

LEFT **Artwork by Detlev van Ravenswaay of the 12 zodiac constellations seen as a fixed imaginary belt round the Earth.**

early astronomy (mapping the stars), astrology (interpreting the stars), magic (manipulating the intelligences behind the stars) and religion (venerating the gods and goddesses associated with the stars).

The geometry determining and connecting these sighting points was heavenly and therefore regarded as sacred in a very real sense. The Babylonians were probably the first people to measure and record the constellations, although this knowledge was available at a very early time to both the Egyptian and Greek civilizations.

Mapping the stars

The fixed stars provide a network on which to plot these movements, and the Zodiac, together with a system of houses, evolved into a detailed map that became very important to astrologers. Incidentally, astrologers were originally concerned with the overall changes in the fabric of the heavenly pattern that in turn affected everybody, rather than being particularly interested in the fate of individuals.

However, because the fixed stars were rotating all the time, the Ancients still found it difficult to take precise measurements unless they could take

measurements at the same instant on the same day in the same season—a clearly impossible task. So they developed constellation groupings to describe the different parts of the heavens and then mapped the stars and planets in relation to these. They measured the relationships between the stars rather than a specific, one-time, positional reference. This was an improvement on merely noting the rising and setting times on the horizon.

For each constellation they recorded the number of visible stars, the particularly bright stars (such as Sirius) and the shape (for example, a bull or an arrow). Initially this was a simple cataloguing process, but later they introduced spherical geometry for more precise recording—and this was truly heavenly geometry at work.

Accurate mapping was important, which is why such huge efforts were put into building astronomically aligned structures in imperishable stone. Examples of these structures include the relatively modern Jantar Mantar in Delhi, the pyramids of ancient Egypt (see pages 117–119) and the huge system of stone and wood circles of ancient Britain and their closely associated ley lines (see pages 96–101), all of which relate to star positions.

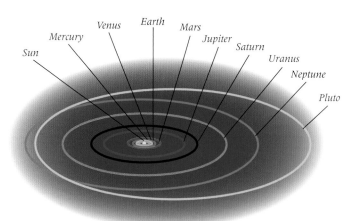

Mercury Venus Earth Mars Jupiter Saturn Uranus Neptune Pluto Sun

RIGHT The planets' paths around the Sun, showing their relative positions and elliptical orbits.

The planets

From an early age the Ancients identified heavenly bodies that moved around the sky in complex paths. These 'wandering stars' are, in fact, the planets, and the ancients knew of five: Mercury, Venus, Mars, Jupiter, and Saturn. They move through the constellations of the Zodiac and, like the Earth, follow elliptical orbits around the Sun. However, their paths appear to be complex because we watch them while standing on a planet that is also moving. As a result, they sometimes seem to go backwards.

Copernicus' breakthrough

Polish astronomer-monk Nicholaus Copernicus (1473–1543) argued in *De revolutionibus orbium coelestium* that the planets and the Earth orbited around the Sun. This was a major breakthrough, but Copernicus proposed circular orbits for the planets following Ptolemy's spheres because he considered the sphere to be a perfect figure and therefore the one God was most likely to choose. Accurate astronomical observations soon began to show that this was not strictly accurate.

Copernicus broke away from the medieval cosmology that made the Earth the center of everything. Of his seven astronomical postulates, the two most important are:

• "The centre of the Earth is not the center of the world [universe], but only of the heavy bodies [the four elements] and of the lunar orb [the Moon]."
• "Every motion that seems to belong to the firmament does not arise from it, but from the [movement of the] Earth. Therefore, the Earth with the elements in its vicinity accomplishes a complete rotation around its fixed pole, while the firmament … remains motionless."

Kepler shows the way

Copernicus still thought in terms of the elements and Aristotle's revolving orbs. Johannes Kepler (1571–1630), a student of one of Copernicus' disciples, established that the paths of the planets are actually ellipses in 1609. But even Kepler harked back to the sacred geometry of the five Platonic solids (see pages 54–55) in order to calculate the distances between the orbits of the planets.

More than 1,900 years after the Greek mathematician Menaechmus (380–320 BC) discovered the ellipse, Johannes Kepler realized that this geometric figure best described the motions of the planets around the Sun. He drew elaborate diagrams of a succession of spheres enclosing each of the Platonic solids, finally enclosing the Earth. Kepler could thus see a way of reconciling Pythagoras with the latest planetary observations, and in a way it was a new version of the old nested-orb theories. He also revived the theory of the harmony of the spheres by associating musical notes with the planetary orbits (see pages 22–23). Like Leonardo da Vinci, Kepler was truly a Renaissance man as well as being a skillful technical astronomer, who wanted to see the geometry of the Ancients still fit with the universal scheme.

Kepler's laws

In 1600 Danish astronomer Tycho Brahe (1546–1601) invited Kepler to work with him in Prague under Rudolph II of Bohemia, whose court sponsored the largest collection of astronomers, astrologers, alchemists, and magicians in Europe, including Dr. John Dee (see pages 93–95). Brahe provided the data that Kepler needed to test his theories. In his first law Kepler showed that a planet moves in an elliptical orbit that has the Sun as one of its two foci. His second law, showed that a line joining a planet to the Sun sweeps out equal areas in equal times, as the planet charts its orbit.

In 1619 Kepler finally figured out that there is just one 'magic' number that gave the answer to both orbit size and timing. His third law states that the ratio of the square of a planet's orbital time is proportional to the cube of its mean distance from the sun:

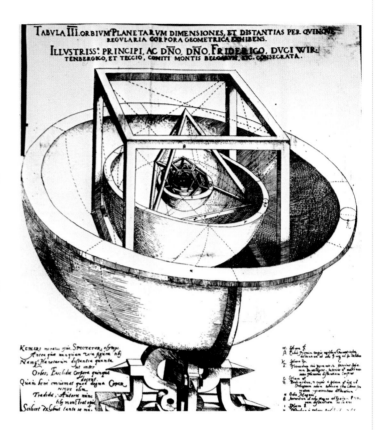

t^2/r^3 = Kepler's constant
(where r = average orbital radius and t = time of 1 circuit round the Sun in days)

ABOVE Kepler tried to use Plato's five perfect solids to determine the spacing of the orbits of the planets, truly applying sacred geometry to astronomy.

Amazingly, even the outer planets that were discovered long after Kepler's death, vary by only a maximum of 0.24 per cent (in the case of Pluto) from this median value. Strangely, you can measure the period and radius in any units you want, as long as you keep them consistent for the whole calculation.

This rule works for the Earth and the outer planets. Again, we have a confirmation that the laws behind the universe are reducible to simple geometry (the ellipse) and simple arithmetic (Kepler's constant).

Significant sky markers

*Among the myriad of stars in the heavens, several key marker stars—
Polaris, Sirius and the Big Dipper—were identified by the Ancients and
used by them for orientation and timing.*

The Pole Star

In the Northern Hemisphere the Pole Star helped ancient peoples to navigate at night by showing them the location of celestial north—the point in the sky directly above the rotational axis of the Earth (see page 75). However, over a very long period of time the Earth 'wobbles' as it spins—like a spinning top. Every 26,000 years it appears that the location of celestial north traces out a rough circle in the sky, a process called precession. This effectively means that the identity of the Pole Star changes very slowly during this time from one star to another nearby star.

If we divide the 26,000 years of this precession of the Pole Star by 12 (the 12 Zodiacal signs) we get a period of approximately 2,166 years. This has prompted astrologers to divide the precession into 12 'ages'—the last 2,000+ years were designated the Age of Pisces, and at present we are witnessing the dawning of the Age of Aquarius, much heralded by hippies and esotericists alike. This has also been seized upon to explain the rise and fall of particular religions. Cultural traces of this precession include the fish as an early symbol of Christianity (Age of Pisces) and the ram as symbolic of the Age of Aries before to the birth of Christ.

This precession means that we can date buildings and historical events by identifying which star was the Pole Star for the cultures of the period. British astronomer Sir John Herschel put forward

ABOVE **The precession of the Zodiac means that the last 2,000 years (the Age of Pisces) have now given way to the Age of Aquarius.**

this suggestion in the middle of the 19th century, and Robert Bauvel developed it in his book *The Orion Mystery* published in 1994 in relation to the pyramids.

In an article published in *Nature* in 2000 Dr Kate Spence, an Egyptologist from the University of Cambridge's Faculty of Oriental Studies, England, attempted to steal the limelight by fixing the precise date of the commencement of the construction of Khufu's Great Pyramid as 2480 BC, about 75 years more recently than was previously thought.

Today, the north celestial pole is marked by Polaris, known technically as α-Ursae Minoris. According to Dr Spence, at the time of the construction of the Great Pyramid the relevant Pole Star belonged to the same constellation and was shared between ζ-Ursae Minoris and β-Ursae Minoris. Their apparent alignment enabled the allocation of a specific date for the foundation of the Great Pyramid.

Sirius

Sirius (or α-Canis Majoris) is without doubt the brightest star in the sky and one of the closest to Earth. Otherwise known as the dog star after the name of its constellation (Canis), it was especially significant for the ancient Egyptians because its heliacal rising heralded the inundation of the Nile and the beginning of the year. As we saw earlier, stars are most easily plotted as they rise and set over the eastern or western horizons. The term heliacal rising refers to the appearance of the star in the few minutes before dawn, before the Sun (Helios) rises and obscures the light of the stars.

The Big Dipper

This constellation, sometimes called the Plough, is close to the Pole Star and in fact points to it. Named after a ladle, not the fairground ride, the Big Dipper is always visible at night in the Northern Hemisphere. It never actually sets below the horizon, but circles around the Pole Star like the hands of a huge clock. Its rotational path can actually be used to tell the time at night or the season of the year. The ancient Chinese venerated this constellation as a time-keeper and pole-pointer, as the home of the nine flying stars of classical *feng shui* and the dark god of the north.

LEFT Heliacal rising occurs when a star rises over the horizon a few moments before dawn.

LEFT The Pole Star, which marks the point in the northern sky around which the rest of the fixed stars appear to rotate.

RIGHT The Big Dipper constellation (shown in yellow), is significant because it acts like a huge time piece, swinging around the Pole Star but always pointing to it (see red line).

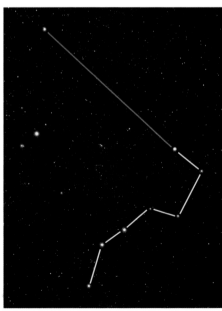

Mapping the world

Cartography, or mapmaking, depends on spherical and projective geometry in order to solve the seemingly insoluble problem of accurately transferring a spherical shape on to a flat representation.

ABOVE **A mariner's brass sextant, which is used to fix the altitude of a heavenly body (Sun, Moon or star) above the horizon.**

BELOW **The map grid applied to the globe. The main latitudinal lines are named, while longitude has only one named meridian, 0 degrees Greenwich.**

Latitudes and longitudes

Abraham Ortelius (1527–1598) and Gerard Mercator (1512–1594) were among the first scientific mapmakers of the 16th century. They consulted mathematicians such as John Dee (see pages 93–95) to help them. To accomplish the transfer from a sphere to a flat surface, they divided the Earth vertically with lines called meridians of longitude and horizontally by lines called parallels of latitude. This meant enclosing every part of the surface of the world in a slightly warped square that could then be replicated on paper. The smaller the square, the more accurate the transference.

The parallels of latitude are, as their name suggests, parallel with each other—

they simply become shorter as they approach the poles. Latitude is simply measured from zero degrees at the Equator to 90 degrees at the poles, using an imaginary right angle at the center of the Earth. As a result, navigators used a sextant and the stars to easily determine the parallel of latitude on which their ship was located.

However, the lines of longitude all converge on the North and South Poles, getting closer together as they do so. This makes longitude much more difficult to measure. The problem of how far around the Earth you had sailed was extremely important for navigators, and many prizes were offered for its solution (a story well documented in Dava Sobel's *Longitude*). As the whole Earth is a sphere, there are obviously 360 possible degrees of longitude or 180 degrees to the west and 180 degrees to the east of the zero longitude. But the problem was where to fix the position of zero degrees longitude.

The prime meridian

Various suggestions for the prime meridian of longitude were made, such as the longitude of Jerusalem, which would have pleased Christian, Jewish and Islamic astronomers, cartographers and geometricians. But there was no logical equivalent of the Equator, which is the position of zero degrees latitude.

In the end the decision came down to politics. The British proposed London (or,

90°
80°
Arctic circle
60°
40°
20°
0°
Greenwich meridian
Tropic of Cancer
Equator
150° 120° 90° 60° 30° 0°
Tropic of Capricorn
Antarctic circle

in fact, Greenwich, which is now a suburb of London), the French proposed Paris and the Americans naturally proposed Washington (I have an old encyclopedia in which maps are drawn with reference to this very short-lived Washington Meridian as a prime meridian).

In 1884, at the International Meridian Conference in Washington, D.C., the Greenwich meridian was adopted as the prime meridian of the world. France abstained. To this day some French cartographers continue to indicate the Paris Meridian (see below) on some maps. The French finally accepted the Greenwich meridian in 1911 (or 1914 for navigation).

The Paris meridian

In 1666 Louis XIV authorized the building of an Observatory in Paris to measure longitude. In the early 1800s the Paris meridian was recalculated by the astronomer François Arago (1786–1853), whose name appears on the 135 plaques that trace its route though Paris.

The line in St. Sulpice, made famous by Dan Brown, is about 91 yards (100 m) from the actual meridian, which passes through the center of the Louvre and its inverted pyramid. The St. Sulpice line is just a gnomon, or shadow line, placed in the church by English clockmaker Henry Sully in 1727 to enable the priest to precisely determine the summer solstice and so calculate the correct date for the celebration of Easter.

In fact, St. Sulpice was the focus of various occult Catholic movements at the end of the 19th century, and was the centerpoint of Joris Karl Huysmans' occult novel *Là-bas*. It is also where the real priest, Sauniere, went to try to find help to

elucidate the parchments he found in his church at Rennes-le-Château in France. For these reasons rather than its Rose Line, which Dan Brown interpreted as the Paris meridian, the church is justly famous.

Henry Lincoln, in his book *The Holy Place*, argues unconvincingly that various ancient structures near Rennes-le-Château are aligned according to the Paris meridian, including medieval churches that were built long before the meridian was even thought of, let alone established. The meridian passes some distance west of the site of the so-called Poussin tomb, an important location in the Rennes-le-Château legend (see pages 150–151).

Measuring time by the Sun and Moon

Time has always been measured in terms of the movement of heavenly bodies, specifically the Sun and the Moon in relation to the Earth. Since the invention of clocks we have become less aware of this.

The basic solar units of time are the day (one revolution of the Earth on its axis) and the year (one revolution of the Earth around the Sun). The basic lunar unit of time is the period from one New Moon to the next.

In Western cultures that rely on tabulated material, such as calendars, people seldom view the Moon as a way of checking the time of the month. In cultures with functional lunar calendars people often go outside their homes to check the phase of the Moon to determine their activities, such as when to plant, pray or break their fast.

Calendars: turning months into a year

There are various ways of measuring the lunar cycle. One 'moon' was always taken to be roughly 29.5 days. In fact, the mean lunar month is 29.531 mean solar days —this is known as the synodical lunar month. However, the lunar month known as the sidereal period (as measured from the stars) is 27.32 days. These two periods are sometimes confused.

Let us use the synodical lunar month of 29.531 days. Twelve such months make 354.372 days, not the 365.256 days of the solar year. Herein lies one of the major calendrical problems of the ancient world and indeed the modern world as well. The Romans tried to solve the problem by stretching the months by various lengths to produce months of 30 or 31 days, thereby filling the year, but getting hopelessly out of step with the actual phases of the moon in the sky.

The Chinese and the Arabs solved the problem by keeping the months tied to the actual observable phases of the moon, with a spare intercalary, or inserted, month every so often just to keep the lunar months roughly in line with the years without reconciling the time periods measured by the Sun and the Moon.

BELOW Earth's stylized orbit round the Sun, showing the different seasons.

The Chinese have perhaps come up with the most practical solution, using two separate calendars that work along side each other: a solar calendar to measure agricultural changes, seasons and *feng shui*; and a lunar calendar to govern magical, ritual and religious concerns.

The prize for the most logical calendar must go to the ancient Egyptians, whose year began with the heliacal rising of Sirius (the day of the first appearance of Sirius at dawn with Helios, the Sun) and had 12 months of exactly 30 days, making 360 days, with 5 days of holiday to make up the full year to 365 days.

The metonic time period

Astronomically, the problem is that the revolutions of the Moon around the Earth do not arithmetically mesh with the revolutions of the Earth around the Sun. The ancient Greeks almost solved the problem by suggesting a metonic time period of 19 years during which the Sun and the Moon catch up with each other before beginning another 19-year cycle. The arithmetic goes like this:

19 years x 365.256 days
= 6,939.86 days
235 synodical lunar months of
29.531 days = 6,939.78 days

Near enough, but still not adequate for measuring really long periods of time. The history of the adjustments that man has made to try to force these two incommensurable numbers into the same calender is complex. Suffice it to say, the geometry of the revolutions of these two heavenly bodies is at the root of all the problems of calculating time.

ABOVE **An engraving of the astronomer Johann Adam Schall von Bell (1591–1666), showing him using Western methods of determining time at the Imperial Observatory in Peking (Beijing). (*Athanasius Kircher, 1668*)**

The hidden connection between time and length

Units of measurement, whether of time or of length, can be derived from nature, astronomy or some other standard. The best and most successful ones are those that are repeatable and easily observed.

Units of measurement

Some of the most notable methods of establishing units of measurement are:

• From natural sources: examples include the size of a barley grain (the kush, a Babylonian unit of volume) and the length of the forearm (the cubit); these can vary considerably in size.
• From an astronomical observation: the rotation of the Earth on its axis (the day) or the Earth's rotation round the Sun (the year).
• From some other standard: for example, the circumference of Earth (see pages 26–27). In fact, this measure is more of a hypothetical calculated one, rather than an physical measure, even today. It is also very difficult to replicate. Inspired by the statement of Aristotle that the

circumference of the Earth was 400,000 *stadia*, it became an article of faith among members of the French *Académie des sciences* in the 18th century that ancient linear measures were all derived directly from fractions of the Earth's circumference and that therefore they should do the same.
• From a standard length: for example, an engraved bar of platinum-iridium, which is used for the yard. However, the standard bar can be kept only at one official location.
• From the swing of the pendulum, which is both a measure of time and of length. Galileo made the extraordinary and counter-intuitive observation that pendulums of the same length will *always* take the same amount of time to execute one swing (this is independent of its weight, the force applied to it or the geometry of its arc). This hidden connection between time and length is easy to measure and simple to replicate anywhere—in fact, it has all the attributes of a suitable international standard.

Standardizing units

In the early 13th century, the authorities in England established a long list of definitions of measurement that were to be used throughout the country. This extremely successful standardization lasted for nearly 600 years, despite a bewildering

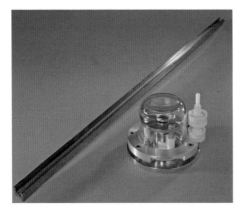

RIGHT **The standard platinum-iridium bar produced by the French government to define precisely the length of the meter. Beside it is the standard kilogram weight.**

array of strange subdivisions, especially for lengths like the rod, pole or perch (these finally dropped out of use in the middle of the 20th century).

The architect and mathematician Sir Christopher Wren (see pages 136–137), who was well aware of sacred geometry, proposed a new system based on the yard, which he defined as the length of a pendulum swing beating at the rate of one per second. The pendulum was applied as a physical timer mechanism in clocks beginning in 1656, although Galileo had already suggested this use as early as 1582.

In France there was no standardization. In fact, the French had approximately 800 different names for measures and, taking into account their different values in different towns, around 250,000 differently sized units.

In an effort to sort this out, Charles de Talleyrand put to the National Assembly in March 1790 a suggestion that a new measurement system be adopted based on a length from nature. The system should have decimal subdivisions, and all measures of area, volume and weight should be linked to the fundamental unit of length. Like Wren, he suggested the basic length should be the length of a pendulum that swings at the rate of one swing per second. This was highly significant because here, in one device, was a standard for both length and time. The proposal was adopted.

However, this proposal was overturned soon after and the opportunity for establishing a truly international standard was lost. In the event, the French settled on the meter, which was fixed to an

erroneous calculation of the circumference of the Earth. Britain and Germany were hostile to the meter and preferred a standard based on the pendulum, and so went their own way.

ABOVE Galileo observed, by watching the swing of this lantern at the Santa Maria Cathedral, Pisa, the time of a pendulum's oscillation relates to its length.

PART 3

THE GEOMETRY OF THE MANMADE WORLD

For thousands of years, architects of sacred structures, such as megalithic circles, Egyptian pyramids and Greek temples, have endeavored to use particular dimensions in their design. These dimensions are whole numbers, geometrically constructable and numerically significant or symbolic. Temples, to whatever god or gods, were conceived as a bridge between man and the deities.

The geometry and the key numbers are not the same in a Gothic cathedral and a Greek temple, but the intention was the same. Some rules of harmony, such as those incorporated into Gothic cathedrals, were dimensions derived from biblical sources. Proportions were specifically intended to bring God closer to human beings. Cathedrals, such as Milan, Chartres and St. Paul's, London, were constructed with significant geometrical measurements and numbers.

In art the geometry of perspective led to the great paintings of the Renaissance, in which the structure of the painting is as carefully planned as that of a building. In the last century the building of harmonic buildings has partially passed from the sacred to the secular.

LEFT **The main pyramid calculation performed by the ancient Egyptians was the calculation of the seked—a measure of the inclination of any one of a pyramid's four triangular faces.**

CHAPTER 5

SACRED GEOMETRY AND THE LANDSCAPE

Ancient megalithic monuments, such as Stonehenge, show how the geometry of the heavens and sacred units of measurement were both applied to the construction of some of man's most impressive temples.

This chapter looks at how the ley system links many megalithic forts, temples and settlements by accurately sighted straight alignments. The study of the relationship between the archaeology of such ancient sites and the astronomical observations they encapsulate has generated a completely new science, that of astro-archaeology.

We examine the changing popular conception of megalithic sites, of which there are thousands scattered across Britain and Europe. Farmers formerly viewed them as a nuisance, then the Romantics saw them as Druidic temples, and in the modern era they are considered by some to be sophisticated observatories, and even predictors, of heavenly phenomena.

Dr. John Dee, an early supporter of the restoration of megalithic sites, was also instrumental in translating Euclid into English and in promoting the geometric study of optics that helped to develop the artistic portrayal of perspective. Finally, we look at the geometry of crop circles, whose complexity in the late 20th century paralleled the work of university mathematicians.

Using geometry to engineer sacred space

Space is sacred when the geometry of its design depends on ratios that are either whole numbers or special, such as the Golden Mean. Sacred space looks and feels harmonious but also has an objective quality, which can be measured and which makes it suitable for a temple.

The ancient Egyptians and ancient Greeks were in no doubt that when they built a temple the measurements had to be consistent with each other and were often round number measures, such as 100 Greek feet or regular submultiples of nine. The volume of the space enclosed was very important, too.

The writings of the Roman Vitruvius, which encapsulated these traditions of building. influenced the later Renaissance building boom. They were, in turn, handed on by architects such as Palladio, who inspired a whole generation of English architects, who produced lovely buildings, such as Chiswick House.

Unanchored geometry

The study of sacred geometry has, however, attracted some pretty strange theories and theorists. As Mario Livio points out in *The Golden Section*, it is possible to draw all sorts of geometric figures over any site plan or any map, but if the major vertices of these do not even fall on actual physical points, intersections or corners, then the conclusions drawn from such a figure are at best arbitrary and at worst complete nonsense. This type of 'unanchored geometry' is particularly popular among many 'New Age' books on sacred geometry.

Unanchored geometry is where unfettered creativity has been used to produce geometric constructions with little of no relevance to the underlying

BELOW **A construction that superimposes a series of unrelated and unanchored *vesica pisces* on the basic rectangular structure of the Parthenon.**

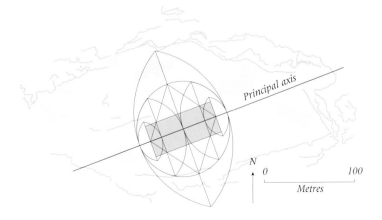

Principal axis

N

0   100

Metres

RIGHT **An example of unanchored geometric interpretation, where only the main axis through Glastonbury Abbey and Dod Lane relates directly to the architecture.**

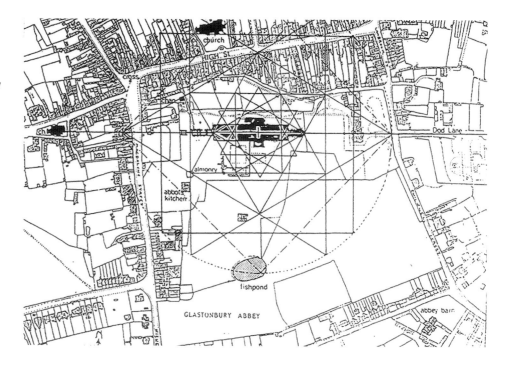

GLASTONBURY ABBEY

structure. Three examples of unanchored geometry spring to mind.

First, the geometric analysis of the Glastonbury Abbey site by a very prolific author: in this construction the line drawn from Dod Lane through the centre of the Abbey and terminating in another church is an obviously valid axis line (and would have been intentional), but the other major vertices all fall on points of little or no significance. For example, one falls just inside the edge of a pond, two appear in private houses, one on Magdalene Street, and one in the middle of a field—none of these are or were significant points.

Second, an elaborate construction of lines and curves producing a *vesica pisces* (see pages 130–131) and other figures (many with their vertices well beyond the structure) have been drawn round the Parthenon (see page 91). Most of the

construction points are in mid-air beyond the platform on which the Parthenon was built, and so cannot have been actually used by the original architect.

Third, the geometric analysis by Lucie Lamy on a plan of the Osirion, which is basically a regular rectangular mortuary temple discovered at Abydos, Egypt, by Flinders Petrie. The geometry is simply that of a rectangular hall with ten square pillars, but a construction of six pentagons inscribed within six circles, diminishing in a wedge shape, has been projected upon it. Of the almost 40 points plotted, only two coincide with a wall and two with a pillar. The rest of the geometry has no connection whatsoever with the structure it purports to interpret. There is no way that the original architect used this fantastic construction to either plan or build the Osirion.

John Dee: Renaissance man

Englishman John Dee was such a Renaissance man that his expertise overlapped many fields—he was a mathematician, geometer, Greek scholar, antiquarian, spy, and sorcerer. He was also involved with the first English translation of Euclid's geometry.

ABOVE John Dee holding a compass and globe to demonstrate his long-standing interests in geometry and mapping.

BELOW Syon House on the Thames outskirts of London, an ancient nunnery before Henry VIII's Dissolution, and home of John Dee's friend the 'Wizard Earl' Henry Percy.

Euclid in English

John Dee (1527–1608) learned Latin and Greek very rapidly, becoming a reader (lecturer) in Greek at Trinity College Cambridge in 1546. His fascination with geometry led him to urge Sir Henry Billingsley to complete the first English translation of the Greek text of Euclid's *Elements* in 1570, to which he added a weighty Preface. The volume was a monumental 928 folio pages and included all the important commentaries on Euclid, from Proclus to Dee himself. It introduced Greek geometry to the English reading public for the first time. In the Preface Dee contends that these arts are based in nature and are therefore sacred, rather than being arbitrary inventions of man.

Preserving antiquity

During Henry VIII's dissolution of the English and Welsh monasteries between 1536 and 1540 some of the finest libraries of manuscripts were destroyed and many stones from these buildings were pillaged. In January 1556 John Dee's passion for preserving the ancient monuments of England prompted him to write a submission to Mary I requesting that she take steps towards, and provide funds for, the preservation of ancient monuments and the manuscripts that had been 'liberated' from the monasteries. He was also conscious that the far older standing stones of pre-Christian Britain (such as Stonehenge) were also disappearing from the landscape and subject to acts of pious destruction by bigoted hammer-wielding clerics.

A frequent traveller between London and Worcester, Dee and his skryer (someone who can see spirits in the crystal), Edward Kelley, became familiar with many of the megalithic sites of southern England—standing stones, ancient stone rings, tumuli barrows and hillforts (Iron Age settlements). In particular he knew in detail Old Sarum (see pages 106–109) and Stonehenge (see pages 110–111).

Dee was also very aware of Glastonbury and the Arthurian legends that surrounded it, as he had attempted to

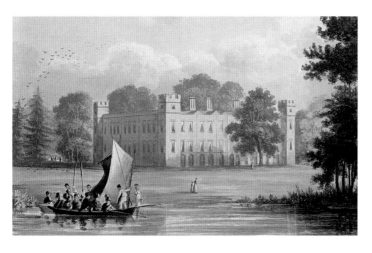

RIGHT **Glastonbury Abbey, a focus for John Dee's interests in ancient monuments, whose abbot, St Dunstan, wrote the alchemical manuscripts discovered by Edward Kelley, Dee's skryer.**

The Glastonbury Zodiac

The so-called Glastonbury Zodiac is often proposed as an example of sacred geometry, and some say that John Dee was the first to make this suggestion. However, despite a supposed quote in Richard Deacon's biography, Dee did not put forward the theory (subsequently promoted by Kathryn Maltwood in 1929) that the outlines of a zodiac were marked out on the ground within a 16 kilometer (10-mile) radius of Glastonbury.

Kathryn Maltwood's interpretation of arbitrary map lines is more that of an artist, whose imagination enabled her to evoke complete images from just the sketchiest of detail than that of a scholar or astronomer. Her theory was a sensation in its day, but enthusiasm for it now is much reduced.

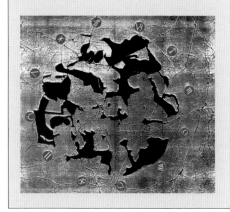

BELOW **The treasure map that Kelley brought to Dee to decipher, and that shows ten ancient sites around Worcester and Glastonbury.**

trace Queen Elizabeth's (and his own) genealogies back to King Arthur. In 1586 Dee's friend William Camden (1551–1623) published his very significant volume *Britannia*, a topographical and historical survey of all the British Isles. Camden's stated intention was 'to restore antiquity to Britaine, and Britaine to its antiquity.' It is a work of chorography: a study that relates landscape, geography, antiquarianism and history.

Buried treasure

Dee's interest in antiquities was more than academic. On 22 March, 1583 Edward Kelley brought him a 'treasure map' (left) showing sketches of ten ancient sites, with their names in code. After a few weeks, Dee broke the cipher, and he and Kelly planned to set out with the intention of recovering some of the treasures. Four of the sites were old stone crosses and one was an Iron Age hillfort, focused around Glastonbury. Such features are often found on ley lines (see pages 96–101), and it is interesting to speculate that Dee's list may have identified key points on one or more such lines.

At Hewitt's Cross, near Northwick, south Gloucestershire, Kelley is reputed to have found a 'red powder', which he and Dee later used to make gold, under well-attested circumstances, in one of the castles of Count Rosenberg near Trebona.

Kelley also found an alchemical book and a scroll said to be by St Dunstan, 'by spiritual direction'—in other words, at the instruction of a spiritual creature. Dee was referring to an angel or a spirit, but often he was unsure of the exact nature of the entity communicating through his crystal, or shewstone. Dee partially deciphered the book, and I have listed (see right) some of the corresponding modern locations, where they are recognizable.

The introduction to the treasure map, which was written in Latin in cipher, and says that the manuscript is the map of treasure buried by Menabon of the Gordanigi (or Menabani of Gordania), who was possibly the chief of a raiding Danish tribe. Glastonbury was actually ravaged by the Danes in the ninth century AD, so this is indeed possible.

Mounteagle's land

Perhaps the most revealing of all of these locations is the central circle marked 'Mounteagles arnid'. This undoubtedly refers to Lord Mounteagle's land, which included Brierley (near Pontefract in South Yorkshire) and Hornby near Lancaster. In 1580, just a few years before this treasure map was found and on the death of William Stanley, the third Lord Mounteagle, their Brierley–Hornby estate was sold. Only the castle and Hornby remained with the Mounteagles, while the Earl of Shrewsbury bought Brierley House for his son, Edward Talbot.

Now this is a curious coincidence, as Dee's main skryer called himself Edward Talbot when he first met Dee, before confessing that his name was really Edward Kelley. I suspect that either Kelley worked for the Mounteagles (and adopted

the son's name at Oxford in order to gain admission) or that maybe he really was the disgraced son of the Earl of Shrewsbury. Interestingly, Shrewsbury is near to Worcester, a continuing focus of interest for much angel skrying from Dee's death to the present day.

Dee's ten treasure sites

Although these ten locations are supposed to be treasure sites, they also show Dee's interest in local monuments, especially the stone crosses, which are often found marking ley lines. Of course, much of Dee's motivation was treasure seeking rather than for scholarly or code-breaking reasons, as he was often short of funds. The sites listed as the treasure sites of Menaban of the Gordanigi were:

- Gilds Cros hic [jacet] meridional iboton = Gilds Cross lying at South Ibboton = Gildas' Cross at Glastonbury.

- Blankes Seters Cross = Blanksetters Cross (modern location unknown).

- Marsars got Cross = Mars God Cross (possible interpretation).

- Huteos Cross = Huets Cross (maybe Hewitts Cross) on Northwick Hill near Blockley, Gloucestershire.

- Fluds Grenul = Floods grenel (possibly the flooded levels near Glastonbury).

- Mons Mene = Mene hill = Meon Hill, Iron Age fort in Warwickshire.

- Mounteagles arnid = Lord Mounteagle's land inherited by Edward Talbot (son of the Earl of Shrewsbury). This was the Brierley estate near Pontefract, Yorkshire.

- Lan Sapant = Land Serpent (possible interpretation).

- Corts nelds = Courts Nelds (modern location unknown).

- Mnpr Merse = Marr merse (modern location unknown).

Alfred Watkins and ley lines

Much has been written about ley lines, but even their modern discoverer Alfred Watkins was unable to say what they are. In 1983 British author, visionary and astro-archeologist John Michell wrote: "Photographic aerial surveys have now been made over much of Britain, and anyone who studies the prints must be struck by the vast number and extent of the regular geometrical lines to be seen both in crop marks and in existing tracks and boundaries."

Watkins's vision

On one hot summer afternoon, 20 June 1921 to be exact, travelling merchant Alfred Watkins (1855–1935) stood on a hilltop at Blackwardine in England and gazed out over the Herefordshire countryside. Suddenly, in a flash of inspiration, he perceived a pattern in the apparently random stretches of roads, field boundaries, rivers, villages and churches—a vast network of what appeared to be

BELOW **Line and cup marks (which may be a sort of ley map) on the pancake stone, at a ley focus on Rombald's Moor, Yorkshire, England.**

straight trackways, linking significant ancient monuments, hillforts, old churches, wayside crosses, hill beacons and manmade dew ponds. He later commemorated this vision in his classic book *The Old Straight Track* (1925).

Anyone who has ridden or wandered around the English countryside, away from the main roads and motorways, will be struck by the meandering pathways and apparent confusion of Victorian village streets, lanes, field boundaries and paths. What Watkins saw was exactly the opposite: he saw straight alignments cutting across the landscape regardless of obstacles. He saw a geometry that no one had seen for hundreds, perhaps thousands of years.

He found that by using large-scale Ordnance Survey maps (and later aerial photographs) he could connect many monuments, churches, cairns, notches cut in the ridges, old high places, holy wells, village ponds, mountain peaks, and Iron Age hillforts along relatively exact alignments. Furthermore, these connected sites turned out to be sites of a specific type—sites that had ancient and pre-Roman pagan significance.

Often, eight or nine sites would line up on just one sheet of a 1:25,000 Ordnance Survey map. Further confirmation of these lines came from aerial photographs, which showed confirmatory marks in crop fields that were not visible from the ground. (These marks can also show up potential archaeological sites and should not be confused with crop circle patterns.) Actually walking along one of these lines often brings to light additional stone markers, ancient earthworks and other features that may not have been recorded on the Ordnance Survey maps.

What are these lines and what were they used for? Watkins and his successors identified a number of clues that help to define their true nature.

Human constructions: the clues

Consistent naming of the places along the lines indicate that they were of human construction rather than natural phenomena. Place names tended to repeat certain syllables in a way that was well beyond statistical chance: villages, features or farms commonly had endings such as '–cole' or '–cold' or '–dod', '–leigh' or '–ley.' Because of this last, Alfred Watkins named them ley lines.

These alignments, these old straight tracks, as Watkins called them, had been overgrown by later additions, cut through by roads, hidden by the creation of village by-pass roads and so on. He was perplexed that even churches seemed to be part of the pattern, until he realized that, as was

LEFT Stonehenge showing two of its trilithons, through one of which passes the major ley line to Old Sarum.

the custom, they had for the most part been built upon older pagan stone circles or groves.

The best Watkins could do was to suggest that they represented old trackways. This theory is untenable because these alignments often led straight through churches, standing stones, across bogs and up gradients that definitely would not have been sensible, or even practical, walking or riding routes.

Other cultures, such as the Inca, had amazingly straight roads, which the king's foot messengers used. The Tibetan *lung-gom-pas* runners also covered long stretches of road at amazing speed. But these should not be confused with leys, any more than *feng shui* dragon veins should be confused with leys.

It is true that the straight Roman roads seemed to follow some of the leys for part of their length, but investigations reveal that often much older, pre-existent tracks lay beneath these roads.

Lines of sight

The ley lines included not only sacred and legendary sites but also high places where beacon fires were lit. The leys were, in fact, lines of sight. They were meant to connect visually the main human settlements and religious and defensive centres of the country to stone circles and Iron Age forts via fairy rings, marker stones and circles built over by churches.

Modern ley hunters tend to accumulate lists of sites along each ley, often trying to extend it as far as possible. However, it is important instead to discover a ley's limits and identify the focus site or terminal point. These focus sites tend to be very obvious at the end of well-marked leys

and are often Iron Age forts (but not burial barrows).

Some of the major leys often take key astronomical bearings from their focus site. For example, the ley that links Grovely Castle, Stonehenge and Sidbury Camp exits out of Stonehenge along the Avenue on the alignment that marks the most northerly rising of the Sun on midsummer day. This tells us that the leys were sometimes an extension of the astronomical geometry of these great stone circles and definitely a product of advanced astronomical measurement and engineering.

Chance alignments?

Some people think that ley lines might simply be an accidental set of coincidental alignments. They believe these chance alignments are what you would expect from the random connection of many thousands of possible points to be found on an Ordnance Survey map or, indeed, in any piece of long-inhabited countryside. This explanation can soon be dismissed by anyone who walks along these ley lines or trackways—they will see a number of additional markers on the exact alignment that would convince even the most hardened sceptic. Alternatively, by applying statistical mathematics (which incidentally includes the use of *phi*) to the alignments that just include major structures, the major ley alignments are shown to be well beyond what you might expect from statistical chance.

Surveying skills

How could pre-Roman people, who, some say, were brutish and backward, do the precise surveying that would be required?

We know the ancient Egyptians built amazingly sophisticated structures 4,500 years ago, so why is it so hard to accept that the inhabitants of Britain were almost equally skilled?

From my geographical background I can assure you that the required surveying was perfectly possible, needing only to use basic equipment, sighting from one wooden staff to another, together with the application of simple geometry, principally the technique of triangulation; see page 100). In fact, there is at least one ancient megalithic alignment from Old Sarum (see pages 106–109) that is so accurate that the modern Ordnance surveyors used this ley line as a baseline to help them correct their readings.

Dragon veins

Some commentators believe that leys involve similar energies to those of the *mei lung*, or dragon veins, of classical Chinese *feng shui*. This cannot be true, because dragon veins pass deep within the Earth and are curved by definition: the *ch'i* energy that travels through the dragon veins must never travel in straight lines but must be nurtured and accumulated by using circuitous paths. Moreover, none of the typical *feng shui* configurations of either water or mountain are found at or near ley termini.

Power lines

An unproven but beguiling explanation is that ley lines are like power-line connections between ancient sacred sites or pagan energy connections. According to the author Paul Devereux, it was the occultist Dion Fortune in her 1936 novel *The Goat-Foot God* who first invented or

BELOW **Glastonbury Tor, standing alone in the middle of low-lying Somerset Levels, in southwestern England.**

The principles of triangulation

Triangulation is the use of triangles by surveyors to map areas accurately. To begin, surveyors measure a certain length exactly to provide a baseline, AB. From each end of this line they measure the angle to a distant point, C, using a surveying instrument called a theodolite, which consists of a small telescope mounted on a plane table designed to measure angles.

The surveyor stands at A and measures the angle CAB, and then stands at B to measure the angle CBA. They now have a triangle in which they know the length of one side and the two adjacent angles. By simple trigonometry they can work out the lengths of the other two sides and hence the exact position of C.

To make a complete survey of the region, they repeat the process, using triangles whose base is the side of the previous triangle. By building on the first triangle they can be sure of each length without having to measure it.

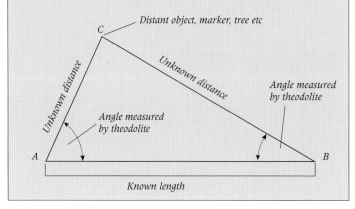

C — Distant object, marker, tree etc

Unknown distance

Unknown distance

Angle measured by theodolite

Angle measured by theodolite

Unknown distance

A

B

Known length

levels, to quote John Michell, from his book *The New View Over Atlantis*: "Yet we still do not know why it is that certain spots on the earth's surface are by general agreement more inspiring than others or how it happens that these very places so often coincide with the centers of prehistoric sanctity."

Very long alignments

Some researchers have identified long, countrywide alignments, but I do not believe these are leys. They are more like corridors than lines and are not nearly as precise as leys, sometimes missing their supposed nodal points by a mile or more. One researcher, Major Tyler, after checking the evidence suggested that it may be best 'to discard the idea of continuous alignments running for long distances' no matter how attractive the idea is.

What ley lines might be

I believe that ley lines are manmade alignments radiating out from major stone circles and earthwork-ringed settlements. They are not natural alignments (as natural features tend to be curved) and are not associated with *feng shui*, UFOs, crop circles or Roman roads (except coincidently). They do not just occur *ad hoc* in the middle of the countryside but were imposed on the British landscape in pre-Roman, possibly Iron Age, times by a culture that could move and erect huge stones and could create large earthworks and ditches. It was a culture that left no written record and few traces of its wooden domestic dwellings.

The principle purpose of ley lines was to link major sites, such as Old Sarum and

popularized the idea that ley lines were 'lines of power' linking prehistoric sites.

Dion, in fact, lived part of the time at the foot of Glastonbury Tor and so had the opportunity to examine alignments at first hand at a time when many of the old landscape features still remained. Glastonbury was, and still is, an undoubtedly spiritual center that it is the focus of several leys. Although the Tor is geographically very arresting, inasmuch as it is a solitary and steep hill amid the surrounding low-lying and waterlogged

RIGHT **The huge central mound of Old Sarum, the focus of ten main leys. Around this lies a further and larger circular earthwork covering 30 hectares (75 acres).**

BELOW **Maiden Castle, an Iron Age fort near Dorchester, Dorset, England, showing a few of its massive manmade earthworks that are part of the culture that engineered the leys.**

Avebury, with other settlements, hillforts, smaller circles and sacred religious sites. The practical limit of a ley is the visible horizon and at most about 35 kilometres (22 miles). Anyone wishing to be convinced that leys once radiated from the sites of stone circles, rather than simply passing through them, should study the Ordinance Survey map showing the landscape north-northwest of the circle at map reference NT 972 205 for a very clear example.

Effectively, the leys formed an intricate and sacred geometry—the geometry of individual sites is related to horizon points that were determined by the rising and setting points of the Moon and the Sun. This geometry creates the magic that ties together the whole land, under the control of one chief, king or priesthood. If this sounds too mystical, then add the additional function of allowing rapid military communication along lines of sight using beacons.

Astro-archaeology

An ancient civilization that flourished in Britain and western Europe in pre-Roman times created megalithic sites, such as Avebury and Stonehenge. The word megalithic literally means 'big stones' and does not indicate an historical period. Archaeologists disagree about the dating of such sites, with many of the ley termini designated as either Iron Age or sometimes from the Neolithic period (40,000–2500 BC).

The Romans made good use of the ready-made defenses of megalithic sites and the straight chariot tracks between them, but until the 16th century stone circles were nothing more than miscellaneous collections of stones—or else the work of giants or magicians. We owe a considerable debt to Dr. John Dee (see pages 93–95), William Camden, John Aubrey and the Reverend William Stukeley (see page 104), who restored the vision of megalithic stones as a significant part of British heritage.

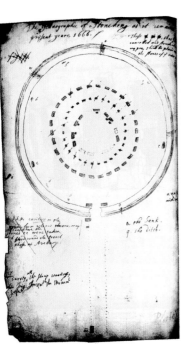

BELOW John Aubrey's plan of Stonehenge, showing the 56 lunar 'Aubrey Holes' and the Avenue leading from the northeast to the main entrance.

A new science is born

We still don't know everything about megalithic sites and the patterns existing between them, despite detailed Ordnance Survey maps, aerial photographs and the diligence of a small band of dedicated astro-archaeologists who, over the course of the 20th century, plotted and measured at least the largest and better known of these monuments.

Perhaps first and foremost was Professor Alexander Thom (see page 105), who probably made the largest number of measurements, but others included Sir Norman Lockyer (see pages 104–105), Gerald Hawkins (1928–2003), the unsung but influential C. A. Newham (1899–1974) and even the renowned astrophysicist Fred Hoyle (1915–2001).

John Michell, probably more than any-one, brought the intricacies and geometric beauty of megalithic sites to the attention of the New Age movement with two books—*The New View Over Atlantis* (1969) and *A Little History of Astro-Archaeology* (1977).

The work done by these researchers showed conclusively that the megalithic sites were constructed with a detailed appreciation both of geometry and of astronomical alignments. The arrangement of the stones plotted the changing positions of both the Sun and the Moon over the course of the year—in the case of Stonehenge, first the lunar positions, then later the solar rising and setting positions. Thom particularly provided a body of careful measurements from hundreds of such sites from Callanish in the northern isles of Scotland to Brittany in France. And so the new science of astro-archaeology was born.

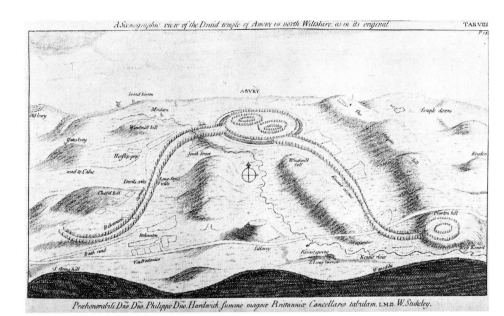

A Scenographic view of the Druid temple of Avury in north Wiltshire, as in its original

ABVRY

TAB VIII

Prehonorabili Dño Dño Philippo Dño Hardwick summo magnæ Britanniæ Cancellario tabulam LMD W Stukeley.

Antiquarian Aubrey at Avebury

When John Aubrey (1626–1697) realized that standing stones, particularly those at Avebury (near where he was born in Wiltshire), were laid out in a geometrical manner he set about recording and mapping the huge structures.

Aubrey's most important contribution to the study of British antiquities was *Monumenta Britannica*, which surprisingly remained unpublished until the 1980s. It contains the results of Aubrey's fieldwork at Avebury and Stonehenge as well as notes on many other ancient sites. The original title of his manuscript was *Templa Druidum*, or the 'Druid's Temples,' reflecting Aubrey's romantic conviction (now seen as incorrect) that the Druids built these megalithic temples.

Aubrey is also remembered for his early plan of Stonehenge (see left), in which he identified a series of slight depressions immediately inside the outer earthworks. These 56 holes were identified between 1921 and 1925 by the Society of Antiquaries as holes cut in the chalk to hold timber pillars, and were named 'Aubrey Holes' in honor of his early observation. These holes, being twice 28 in number, almost certainly relate to the lunar cycle of 28 days, or the 28 mansions of the Moon. They belong to the earliest first phase of construction when Stonehenge was made of timber rather than the stone megaliths.

Avebury

The Avebury complex of standing stones and avenues, which covers about 11.33 hectares (28 acres), is thought to date from 2500 BC. The village of Avebury was built on the crossroads in the middle of the site without respect to the original stones, which were often reused in walls or else destroyed.

The megalithic site is made up of a huge circular earthwork ditch, which was originally about 366 yards (9.15 meters)

deep, and a bank about 0.25 miles (400 m) in diameter. I speculate that this was initially intended to hold water, although it is now dry after being breached long ago. This ditch encloses an outer circle of large standing stones, which has entrances at four points that roughly align with the cardinal points of north, south, east, and west. Radiating from the large circle were two avenues of stones.

Inside the outer circle are two smaller inner circles, both about 340 feet or 125 megalithic yards (103.6 m) in diameter. The northern inner circle consisted of two concentric circles—the inner one had 12 stones (for solar measurement) and the outer one had 27 stones (possibly for lunar measurement)—

surrounding three very large central stones. At the center of the southern inner circle stood a tall stone over 20 feet (6.1 m) in height, which was destroyed at some time in the last two centuries.

Reverend William Stukeley

Dr William Stukeley (1687–1765) was inspired by John Aubrey's discoveries but his romanticism furthered the Druid association with megalithic sites and added the fantasy of a supposed dragon or serpent cult. During his many visits, he saw the destruction of numerous standing stones by farmers using large hammers and fire, intent on either clearing the land or destroying pagan remains. The titles of his best-known books, *Stonehenge, a Temple Restored to the British Druids* (1740) and *Avebury, a Temple of the British Druids* (1743), clearly show his Druidic focus. The New Age Druid movement owes much of its origins to his romantic tales.

Sir Norman Lockyer

Sir Norman Lockyer (1836–1920) was the world's first professor of astronomical physics at the Royal College of Science, London, which is now part of Imperial College. He also founded and edited the prestigious scientific journal *Nature*. Lockyer was interested in the measurement and alignment of temples of many cultures, not just Britain's.

In 1890 Lockyer noticed that numerous ancient Greek temples were aligned along a generally east–west axis. He worked with F.C. Penrose, who made the most precise measurements of the Parthenon (see pages 124–127), and investigated potential alignments with the position of sunrise on specific days. In Egypt he found

BELOW Eighteenth-century surveyors using a simple theodolite and measuring staff to survey, just as their Iron Age predecessors did before them.

alignments connected with the star Sirius (see pages 80–81), whose heliacal rising heralded the beginning of the Egyptian year. He published these theories in *The Dawn of Astronomy* in 1894.

At Stonehenge Lockyer assumed that the Sun at midsummer must originally have risen over the marker called the Heel Stone, and he calculated this date—and hence the date when Stonehenge was built—using current astronomical data. He extended these ideas to other megalithic sites and published his conclusions in *Stonehenge and Other British Monuments Astronomically Considered* in 1906. As a result, he is sometimes called the 'father of archaeo-astronomy.'

Alexander Thom and the megalithic yard

As a professor of civil engineering, Alexander Thom (1894–1985) was accustomed to precision measurement, and he used the statistical results from hundreds of sites to validate his theories. Thom's data are still accepted, but his conclusions are controversial.

In 1934 Alexander Thom became interested in megalithic circles and their astronomical alignments. He understood that the engineers who raised such huge structures must have been well versed in astronomy and geometry as well as inengineering. Thom set about accurately surveying and measuring megalithic sites throughout Britain and published the initial results in 1955 in *The Journal of the Royal Statistical Society*.

His most startling conclusion was that the megalithic rings had been laid out according to a standard unit of measure-ment that he called the megalithic yard.

He estimated that this unit was equivalent to 2.72 feet (0.83 m). In his book *Megalithic Sites in Britain* he shows the results of his surveys of some 300 megalithic circles, alignments and isolated standing stones.

The megalithic yard relates to the 'measuring rod,' a very old British unit of length. Also known as the pole or perch, the rod measures 16.4 feet (5 m). This is slightly more than 6 mega-lithic yards (2.722 x 6 = 16.332 feet). Interestingly, the square rod measures an area of 6 x 6 megalithic yards. Could it be that the rod is the last remaining trace of the megalithic yard used by the megalithic builders as a standard measure?

Although not everyone is satisfied with Thom's values, there can be no doubt that complex geometry and standardized measurements were key in the construc-tion of these huge monuments.

ABOVE The megalithic stones of Callanish on the Isle of Lewis in Scotland, where Alexander Thom had his first taste of stone circle surveying.

Old Sarum: the focus of many ley lines

The keys to the meaning and disposition of ley lines are the nodes from which they radiate. Often, however, there will be one prime meridian ley among a number radiating from a particular site. One good example is the leys that radiate from Old Sarum in the English county of Wiltshire.

BELOW A cathedral was originally built on Old Sarum, before its destruction caused its relocation to Salisbury, which is still on the same ley line.

Old Sarum is a flat-topped earthwork with a commanding view of Salisbury Plain and the River Avon, which cuts through the plain and flows towards it. The main earthworks and ley alignments were constructed in pre-Roman times. Old Sarum has been the focus for settlement for a long time—first as an Iron Age hillfort, a Roman encampment and then a medieval walled city.

In 1070, William the Conqueror's troops disbanded here after their conquest, prompting the bishop of St Osmund to build a new cathedral at Old Sarum, which was consecrated in 1092. But the pagan energies of the place reasserted

themselves, and, just five days later, a great storm gathered and the building was largely destroyed by lightning. Despite its subsequent reconstruction, the cathedral was never very successful and was finally relocated to nearby Salisbury in 1220, but still on the same ley alignment.

The Old Sarum–Stonehenge ley

All the main leys associated with Old Sarum radiate to the north, fanning out to the northeast and northwest. One ley, perhaps the most famous of them, passes through Stonehenge and then continues to the south through Salisbury Cathedral, Clearbury Ring and Frankenbury Camp (both Iron Age hillforts).

This particular ley runs for at least 17.3 miles (27.8 km) north-northwest to south-southeast. Some researchers have suggested also that it continues to the south coast of England. It is certainly the prime meridian ley through Old Sarum, and it was originally noticed by Sir Norman Lockyer (see pages 104–105).

The ley line may originate in the tumuli at Durrington Down before running through the center of Stonehenge and Old Sarum to the rebuilt spire of Salisbury Cathedral, located to the south of its original site at Old Sarum. Strangely (according to Guy Underwood, a prolific British author on ley lines) this tower marks a blind spring that seems to attract unnaturally large swarms of insects and birds, a phenomenon often associated with a ley focus.

The line then crosses old Harnham bridge over the River Avon and passes precisely through a major crossroads (A338 and A354), both common ley line features. It then passes down the old straight Odstock road and on to Clearbury Ring, which is a wooded, Iron Age camp that can be seen from miles around. The ley then passes the remains of the 12th-century priory of Breamore and terminates in the Iron Age Frankenbury Camp (near Fordingbridge), interestingly a site where much UFO activity has been sighted in the recent past.

Other Old Sarum leys

There are nine other major leys radiating to the North of Old Sarum, but none of these has southwards extensions. It is almost as if Old Sarum was meant to be in command of the whole Salisbury Plain to its north, in either a religious or military sense. This example well illustrates how leys relate to surrounding features.

At least two of the leys follow old Roman roads (leys 1 and 3), while all nine terminate in rings, camps, Iron Age forts or cathedrals.

The key to the original use of the leys probably lies in understanding what their terminals were. If these terminals were only forts, it strongly suggests a military communication function, such as beacon lines of sight. If, however, these forts were also busy trading settlements, then a travelers' line of sight function is a possibility, even if the road did not always follow it. Lastly, if they were religious sites, then we have seriously to consider a deliberate geometrical interlocking of spiritual energy points. Let us look at a few of these terminals:

• At Figsbury Ring (ley 2) one entrance frames a view of Old Sarum, showing its connection with Old Sarum.
• Portway Roman road (ley 3) linked Silchester directly to Old Sarum.

North

Stonehenge

Old Sarum

Salisbury Cathedral

Harnham Bridge (over River Avon)

A338 and A354 Major crossroad

Clearbury Ring

Breamore Priory

Frankenbury Camp

South

ABOVE A diagram showing the sites connected by the main ley passing through Old Sarum and Stonehenge (not to scale).

• Sidbury Camp (ley 4) is also located on the major Grovely Castle–Stonehenge–Sidbury Camp ley.

• Ogbury Camp, Woodhenge and Durrington Walls (ley 5) are significant sites, the former covering 2.55 hectares (63 acres) with ramparts 33 feet (10 m) high. Woodhenge is older than Stonehenge, and Durrington Walls is Britain's largest henge site.

• Ley 6 is the main ley passing through Old Sarum and also through Stonehenge. Its southeast extension is obviously at 171 degrees (351 degrees—180 degrees = 171 degrees). Avebury Ring is also close to this alignment at 354 degrees.

LEFT **Snow helps to define the ditches and banks surrounding Yarnbury Castle, an Iron Age fort and the terminus of ley (number 7) from Old Sarum.**

THE TEN MAIN LEYS RADIATING OUT FROM OLD SARUM

Ley number	Grid bearing from Old Sarum	Distance from Old Sarum (in miles)	Ley aimed at or aligned with	Type of terminus feature
1	84°		Roman road towards Dunstable Pond	Roman road, dew pond
2	78°	3.25	Figsbury Ring	Ring
3	55°	9.80	Portway Roman Road leading to Quarley Hill then Silchester	Roman road, Iron Age fort, pre-Roman town
4	23°	12.00	Sidbury Camp	Iron Age fort
5	6°	3.50, 6.00 7.00	Ogbury Camp, Woodhenge, Durrington Walls	Iron Age fort, ring, henge
6	351°	6.00	Stonehenge	Ring
	171°	2.00, 5.30, 11.30	Salisbury Cathedral, Clearbury Ring, Frankenbury Camp	Cathedral, ring, Iron Age fort
7	307°	8	Yarnbury Castle	Iron Age fort
8	297°	10.90	Codford Circle, Wilsbury Ring	Ring, ring
9	89°	6.00	Grovely Castle	Iron Age fort
10	286°	8.30	Bilbury Ring	Ring

These leys can be clearly seen on the 1:25,000 Salisbury and Stonehenge Ordnance Survey Explorer Map 130.

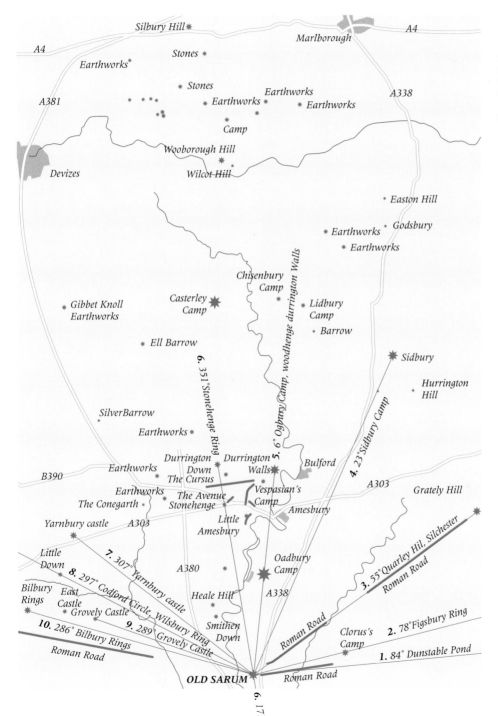

Silbury Hill *
Marlborough
A4
A4
Stones *
Earthworks *
A381
Stones *
Earthworks * Earthworks
Earthworks *
Earthworks *
A338
Camp
Wooborough Hill
Devizes
Wilcot Hill

Easton Hill *
Earthworks * Godsbury
Earthworks *

Chisenbury
Camp
Gibbet Knoll
Earthworks
Casterley
Camp
Lidbury
Camp
Barrow *

Ell Barrow *

Sidbury *
Hurrington
Hill *

6. 351°Stonehenge Ring

5. 6° Ogbury Camp, woodhenge durrington Walls

4. 23°Sidbury Camp

SilverBarrow
Earthworks *

Durrington Durrington
B390 Earthworks Down Walls Bulford
The Cursus
Earthworks Vespasian's A303 Grately Hill
The Conegarth * The Avenue Camp
Stonehenge Amesbury
Yarnbury castle A303 Little
Amesbury
7. 307° Yarnbury castle
Little Oadbury
Down **8.** 297° Codford Circle, Wilsbury Ring Camp **3.** 55°Quarley Hil, Silchester
Bilbury A380 A338 Roman Road
Rings East Heale Hill
Castle Clorus's **2.** 78°Figsbury Ring
10. 286° Bilbury Rings * Grovely Castle Smithen Camp
9. 289° Grovely Castle Down Roman Road **1.** 84° Dunstable Pond
Roman Road

OLD SARUM * Roman Road

6. 171°

Stonehenge: the crossing of two main leys

Stonehenge may be the most famous megalithic circle in Britain, but only two major leys pass through it (although Alexander Thom has suggested a third). These two leys are clearly marked by physical features at Stonehenge, the Avenue and two isolated stones.

The Stonehenge–Old Sarum ley

Stonehenge is, in fact, a completely different type of structure from, and much smaller in size than, Old Sarum. At its simplest, the basic orientation of Stonehenge is northeast, looking between the Heel Stone and another missing stone, up the Avenue (a processional way) towards Sidbury Camp, some 7.75 miles (12.4 km) away.

The first defining ley has a grid bearing of 351 degrees from Old Sarum (see page 108) and passes directly through Stonehenge. Its entry and exit points are clearly marked by the station stones 92 and 94 set on two mounds and placed diametrically opposite each other. These two markers can clearly be seen in the illustration (see right).

The Stonehenge–Grovely Castle ley

The second defining ley passes through Stonehenge at grid bearing 49 degrees. Its entry point is clearly marked by the Avenue. It links Stonehenge with Castle Ditches (a large Iron Age hillfort and settlement) and Grovely Castle (an Iron Age monument) to the southwest and Sidbury Camp (an Iron Age monument) to the northeast. The direction of this ley closely approximates the northeasterly position of sunrise on the longest day of the year (midsummer), a popular time for people to gather at the stones.

This ley line was originally pointed out by Sir Norman Lockyer (see pages 104–105) and is 22 miles (35.2 km) long, making it one of the longest genuine leys. Colonel Johnstone, previously director general of Ordnance Survey, pointed out that he used this ancient alignment as a baseline with which to improve the accuracy of the Ordnance Survey maps.

The two leys intersect at exactly the centre of the Sarsen circle at Stonehenge. The so-called Slaughter stone is located just inside where the 'ghost path' and the ley (see right) enters the earthwork enclosure of Stonehenge. Likewise, the horseshoe-shaped group of 10 trilithons faces receptively towards this northeast entrance. Whatever its purpose, Stonehenge was definitely focused along the northeasterly Avenue, either from the King Barrows or from the River Avon.

The path of the Avenue

The Avenue leads out of Stonehenge at a 49-degree grid angle (northeast) and proceeds for roughly 4,700 feet (1,432 m) where it crosses at right angles the highly significant King Barrows ridge. It then proceeds for another 4,700 feet (1,432 m) to the banks of the River Avon, changing

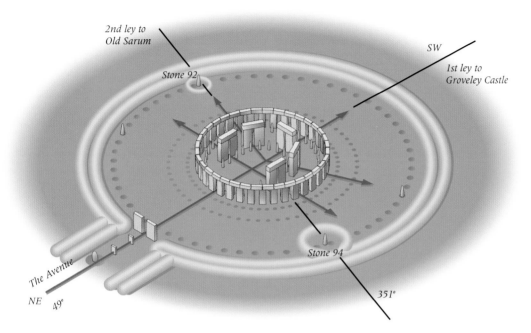

*2nd ley to
Old Sarum*

Stone 92

SW

*1st ley to
Groveley Castle*

The Avenue

NE 49°

Stone 94

351°

ABOVE **Perspective view of
Stonehenge showing the
crossing of its two main leys
and their stone markers.**

its course to 97 degrees (east) and then finally to 159 degrees (southeast) before reaching the river.

It is possible that the path of the Avenue mimics the movement of the Sun through the year, rising in the northeast at midsummer, then east during spring and autumn and finally southeast at mid-winter. So the apparent bent shape may have a clear geometric link with the perceived movement of the position where the Sun rises throughout the year.

The significant thing is that this ghost path was exactly bisected at right angles by the burial feature of the King Barrows. Admittedly, it is only one of many burial barrows in this area, but its name suggests a certain precedence—it also runs north–south across the Avenue rather than in the more usual east–west direction of a burial barrow.

Meeting the dead

If you compare Stonehenge's layout with the rules of the Chinese practice of *feng shui*, you will see that it has entrances rather like the gates of *feng shui*. These are usually listed as northeast, the Gate of Ghosts or ancestors, northwest, the Gate of Heaven, southwest, the Gate of Man and southeast, the Gate of Earth. These are located at each of the intercardinal points. In the context of Stonehenge, the Avenue is the main entrance, and it coincides with the Gate of Ghosts.

It seems to me that apart from the undoubted astronomical alignments of the geometry of Stonehenge, one of the basic uses might have been as a ritual or sacred space for the living to meet with the dead, or their honored ancestors.

Labyrinth and mazes

Labyrinths and mazes are often confused as the terms are not used consistently. Labyrinth implies a permanent structure, usually with a specific or symbolic purpose, while mazes tend to be more temporary, life-size structures often constructed of hedge or fences.

Hedge mazes are fairly recent 17th century introductions and some remain at English stately homes, such as Chatsworth and Longleat. Once the playthings of the landed gentry, mazes became tourist attractions and are proliferating. Longleat is home to no fewer than seven mazes, and the famous Hampton Court maze boasts 300,000 annual visitors.

Ancient labyrinths

It is said that Daedalus built the first labyrinth for King Minos of Crete as a prison for the Minotaur, a half-bull, half-human creature. Minos demanded the regular tribute of 14 youths from Athens to be sacrificed to the Minotaur. However, Theseus hit upon a plan to slaughter the Minotaur and release the Athenians from this grisly tribute. The palace at Knossos has, because of its complex honeycomb architecture, sometimes been identified with the labyrinth, but there are much older examples.

Probably the oldest labyrinth was to be found in Egypt, near Crocodilopolis (Arsinoe). Herodotus (Book 2:148) described it: "I have personally seen it, and it defies description … the labyrinth outstrips even the pyramids. It has twelve roofed courtyards, six in a row to the north and six with their entrances directly opposite them … the labyrinth has rooms on two levels—an underground level and an above-ground level on top of it—and there are three thousand rooms in all … the upper rooms, which I personally saw, seem almost superhuman edifices. For instance, the corridors from chamber to chamber and the winding passages through the courtyards are so complicated that they were a source of endless amazement."

Sadly, this structure has not been definitely located by modern Egyptologists, although it could be the mortuary temple of Amenemhet III at Hawara near Fayyum. Pliny confirms that it was the pattern for the Cretan one: "There is no doubt that Daedalus adopted

RIGHT **A medieval drawing of the classical unicursal labyrinth, with Theseus and the Minotaur battling at its center.**

ABOVE The world's longest hedge maze at Longleat House, Warminster, Wiltshire. It was laid out in 1975 by Greg Bright, with many irregular twists and turns.

it as the model for the labyrinth built by him in Crete, but that he reproduced only a hundredth part of it containing passages that wind, advance and retreat in a bewilderingly intricate manner."

Unicursal labyrinths

A possible derivation of the word 'labyrinth' is from the word *labrys*, a double-headed ritual axe found in the Minoan ruins of Knossos. But this structure bears little relationship to what is today referred to as a unicursal (single line) labyrinth, which does not require any great thought to negotiate—it is a 'walk-through,' single-passageway maze with no junctions or decision points.

Until about AD1000 just one archetypal unicursal labyrinth design prevailed throughout Europe, which is (probably incorrectly) referred to as the Cretan type. It is an interesting piece of geometry and consists of seven annular (ring) paths contained within eight barrier lines, looping backwards and forwards within four quarters created by the original central cross. It is quite possible that these seven layers corresponded to the seven spheres of the classical planets radiating out from the Earth at the center.

Unicursal labyrinths can also be found with square, round or octagonal outlines. They were even found as floor motifs in a number of late medieval French churches. However, all such examples have been destroyed or covered up, with the exception of the one at Chartres Cathedral (see pages 134–135). Here it still functions as a symbol or practical test of Christian penitential devotion but is also walked by an increasing number of New Age seekers. Christian church labyrinths tended to have 11 rings rather than the classical seven.

Interest in mazes and labyrinths has accelerated since the 1970s, and New Age enthusiasts create mazes and unicursal labyrinths—often drawn on floorcloths, cut into turf or made of stones—and walk around them, an act said to generate particular spiritual benefit.

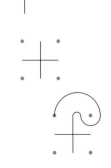

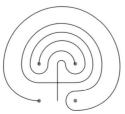

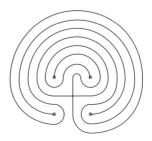

LEFT How to draw a unicursal maze starting with a cross and then progressively joining the dots.

The geometry of crop circles

In August 1980 the first crop circle was discovered in Wiltshire, England, although some researchers report that the phenomenon existed before that date. It was 60 feet (18.3 m) in diameter and based entirely on Euclidean geometry, as indeed are most crop circles.

A year later, another three circles appeared. From then on the number and complexity of such circles has increased almost exponentially, with 120 circles recorded between 1980 and 1987, and 112 in 1988 alone. At its peak, there were over 1,000 reported in 1990—whatever causes crop circles was very busy that year.

The form of crop circles

Crop circles have to be viewed from above to appreciate the designs. The basic form is created by bending over (often without breaking) the stalks of a cereal crop in such a way as to leave no trace. The stalks inside a crop circle are typically bent into a swirl pattern that spins either clockwise or counterclockwise. In multicircular patterns, one circle may spin clockwise and another counterclockwise. Even a single circle may contain two 'layers' of stalks, each spinning in a different direction.

Crop circles can range in size from a metre to a few hundred meters across. Most crop circles were simple circular designs until 1990 when they became more elaborate, and complex crop patterns with intelligent pictograms emerged. The geometry involved in many of the crop circle designs is as complicated as any sacred geometry, either manmade or occuring in nature.

What causes them?

Many theories have tried to explain the phenomenon of crop circles. These include aliens in UFOs, drunken midnight revellers and descending electrically charged whirlwinds. Of course, there have been obviously hoax copies, but the fact remains that these are highly sophisticated geometrical formations and they are often generated in the course of a single night. Some of the geometry is very advanced and unlikely to have been known to hoaxers, unless they were also university maths lecturers.

Having originated in and been most prevalent in Wiltshire, especially near ancient sacred sites, such as the Avebury circle and Silbury Hill, crop circles have begun to appear in other countries, such as the USA, Australia and Russia.

Center for Crop Circle Studies

Sadly, after 15 years of enthusiasm and varied fortunes, the Center for Crop Circle Studies (CCCS) closed itself down for good in October 2005. It passed its considerable archive of records covering most of the history of crop circle research to that worthy Victorian body, the Society for Psychical Research. It is interesting that it did not pass its records to the Meteorological Office or some other purely scientific body.

LEFT **The Windmill Hill crop circle formed near Avebury in 1996, an amazing feat of geometric drafting, difficult to fake without an aerial perspective.**

BELOW **A crop circle at Woodborough Hill, Alton Barnes (2000), reminiscent of the natural spiralling geometry of pine cone scale bracts.**

Interesting physical phenomena have been associated with the sites of crop circles. These include magnetic anomalies, interference with electrical equipment, such as video recorders and phones, and high-pitched sounds. Salisbury Plain in Wiltshire is home to both a number of military installations (suggesting a human but high-technology cause) and is also the site of many ancient stone circles and precision ley lines (see pages 96–101). This suggests an origin connected to the ancient ley energies of the area.

Crop seed samples taken from circles tend to germinate more vigorously than seeds from the rest of the field, and the bend in the stalks seem to be altered at a cellular level rather than being crudely broken as they would by a prankster's walkboard.

Rapid daytime formation

One Sunday afternoon in July 1996, within a 45-minute period, a huge 915 feet (279 m) wide spiral consisting of 151 circles appeared in full view of the busy A303 road, opposite Stonehenge in Wiltshire. A pilot flying over, a gamekeeper and a security guard all confirmed that it had not been there before 5.30pm, yet by 6pm this massive formation was spotted by passing tourists. This proves that not all crop circles are made overnight and that, in this case at least, the circle was constructed much faster than any pranksters could possibly have managed with walkboards.

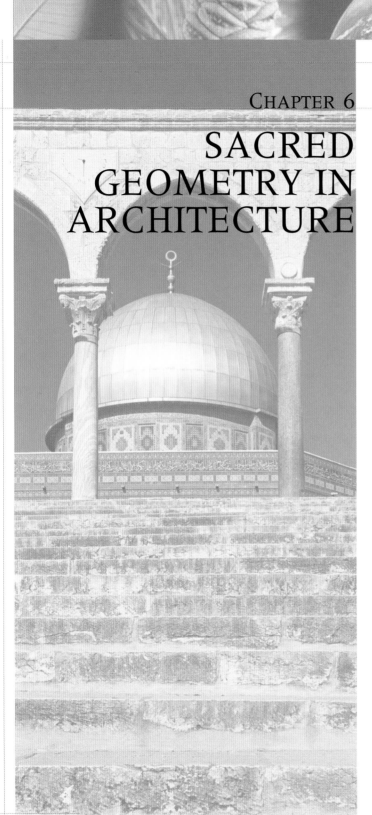

CHAPTER 6

SACRED GEOMETRY IN ARCHITECTURE

This chapter surveys some of the major buildings that incorporate sacred geometry, such as the Egyptian pyramids and Solomon's Temple. The classical lines of the Parthenon embody a geometry so complex that its builder felt the need to write a book about it and yet so simple that it is summed up in just a few numbers.

We look at how the Romans carried on the tradition of sacred geometry and how the real nature of Leonardo da Vinci's Vitruvian man was simply an exercise in determining the relationship between the cubit and the dimensions of the perfect man.

The dimensions of Solomon's Temple discovered by the crusaders inspired the construction of Gothic cathedrals across Europe. We look in detail at the geometry of Chartres Cathedral, with its symbolic floor labyrinth, and at designs drawn for the façade of Milan Cathedral that are based on a series of concentric circles spaced at even and significant intervals. In England, Sir Christopher Wren constructed St. Paul's Cathedral, incorporating archetypal solar numbers, such as 666 and 365, into its structure.

Finally, the movement to make buildings from more organic shapes has passed the torch of sacred construction from religious bodies back to secular architecture.

The geometry of the pyramids

The subject of pyramids makes most people think only of the Great Pyramid and its immediate neighbors. In fact, the Great Pyramid is simply the largest of a succession of more than 35 pyramids, stretching over a long period of Egyptian history.

Despite the apparent similarity between pyramids, there has been some experimentation in slope, height and base length. One pyramid, the Bent Pyramid, even changes its slope half way up. Modern figures for the height of a pyramid are sometimes speculative because calculating the height and gradient of a structure that has lost its capstone and much of its casing appears geometrically simple but can in practice be problematical. Where there is some uncertainty I have provided the closest round number of royal cubits, while staying within the margin of accuracy defined by the modern surveyor.

The seked

The main pyramid calculation performed by the ancient Egyptians is the calculation of the seked. If you check the seked for all the pyramids you will find a range of values, from 3.5 (Iput I) to 7.7 (Senusret II), but two groups clearly stand out: those pyramids with a seked of exactly 5.25 and those with a seked of exactly 5.5. It is interesting that pyramids with the same seked are also geographically close.

Calculating the seked

It seems from the Egyptian Rhind mathematical papyrus that there were a number of basic arithmetic problems, including calculating the gradient (or seked) of a pyramid. One such problem was: If the height of a pyramid is 8 cubits and the base is 12 cubits, what is its seked?

The seked of a pyramid is a measure of gradient or the inclination of any one of its four triangular faces to the horizontal plane of its base. For this exercise we will use a royal cubit where:

1 royal cubit = 7 palms = 28 fingers

The seked is usually expressed as so many horizontal palms per one vertical cubit rise—in modern geometric parlance, the cotangent of the angle of slope of the triangular faces.

To work out the answer to the Rhind problem we simply need to draw the right-angled triangle FEH. Remember that the distance FE is the same as half the base length, or half DA:

Height = 8 cubits.
Half Base = ¹²⁄₂ = 6 cubits.
Expressed in palms
= 7 x 6 = 42 palms
Therefore, the seked = ⁴²⁄₈
= 5.25 palms = 5 palms and 1 finger

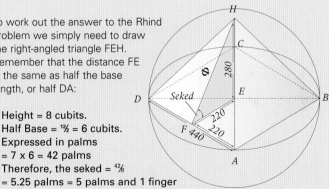

This figure is the correct answer given in the papyrus. Three other problems in the same papyrus were based on the same 5.25 seked ratio, demonstrating its importance in the pyramid design.

THE PYRAMIDS AND THEIR DIMENSIONS

Pyramid or Pharaoh	Location	Length of base (meters)	Height (meters)	Gradient (height divided by base/2)	Length of base (cubits)	Height (cubits)	Seked (base x 7 divided by height x 2)
Userkaf	Saqqara	73.27	48.84	1.333	140.00	93.33	5.2500
Pepi I	Saqqara	77.98	51.98	1.333	149.00	99.33	5.2500
Teti	Saqqara	78.50	52.33	1.333	150.00	100.00	5.2500
Djedkare	Saqqara	78.50	52.33	1.333	150.00	100.00	5.2500
Pepi II	Saqqara	78.50	52.33	1.333	150.00	100.00	5.2500
Khafre	Giza	215.09	143.39	1.333	411.00	274.00	5.2500
G 3a	Giza	43.96	27.97	1.273	84.00	53.45	5.5000
G 1c	Giza	46.05	29.31	1.273	88.00	56.00	5.5000
G 1a	Giza	46.05	29.31	1.273	88.00	56.00	5.5000
G 1b	Giza	48.15	30.64	1.273	92.00	58.55	5.5000
Niuserre	Abusir	78.50	49.95	1.273	150.00	95.45	5.5000
Menkaure	Giza	104.67	66.61	1.273	200.00	127.27	5.5000
Snefru	Meidum	143.92	91.58	1.273	275.00	175.00	5.5000
Khufu	Giza	230.27	146.53	1.273	440.00	280.00	5.5000

From the table of pyramids above we can see that the two most popular seked ratios for pyramids were:

• 5.25—seen in the pyramids of Userkaf, Pepi I, Pepi II, Khafre, Teti, and Djedkare.
• 5.50—seen in the pyramids of Khufu, Snefru, Menkaure, Niuserre, and the four little pyramids at Giza.

These two sekeds are based on simple, whole-figure ratios: seked 5.25 is based on a height:base ratio of 2:3; and seked 5.50 is based on a height:base ratio of 7:11. All sekeds are based on such straightforward, whole-figure ratios.

Assessing the exact height

These sekeds are neither arbitrary nor approximate. Therefore, it is useful to 'back engineer' the height of some of these pyramids using the exact seked and the base measurement (which is usually more precise to measure than the height).

• The seked of 5.25 was based on the Pythagorean triangle with sides of 3:4:5 (see page 17).
• The seked of 5.50 is based on the geometry of the circle.

Now let's look at how this is so. However, in order for it to make sense we should examine two other facts of geometry: the division of the royal cubit into 7 palms and the value of *pi*, π, when establishing the area and circumference of a circle.

First, the division of the royal cubit. The division of a royal cubit into 7 x 4 = 28 digits is a parallel to the 28 lunar mansions. However, as 7 is a prime and a magical number it seems rather strange to use it as a measurement of length because it cannot be divided evenly by any other number. In other measurement systems lengths are usually divided by, for example, 2, 4, 8, 10, or 12. With such systems it is easier to divide up things into halves or thirds. But the ancient Egyptian royal cubit has no such simple division. We shall see why in a minute.

Pyramid dimensions relate to the circle and 7/11

It is said that the distance around the base of the Great Pyramid exactly equals the circumference of a circle whose radius is the height of the pyramid. Let's do the problem in cubits:

Distance round base (ABCD)
= 4 x sides = 4 x 440 = 1760
Circumference of a circle = $2 \pi \times r$
= $2 \pi \times$ height = $2 \times 22/7 \times 280 = 1760$

Now, the value of *pi*, π, as used in calculating the area and circumference of a circle. Today we struggle with the unending decimal 3.1416 … to represent this value. But by using simple whole numbers we can represent it by 22/7. Let us use this value to extend and simplify these formulae:

Area of a circle = $\pi \times r^2 = {}^{22}\!/_{7} \times r^2$
Circumference of a circle = $2\pi \times r$
= $2 \times {}^{22}\!/_{7} \times r$
= $r \times {}^{44}\!/_{7}$

Therefore, a circle with a radius of 7 cubits = $7 \times {}^{44}\!/_{7}$ = 44 cubits circumference. Which means (dividing both sides of the equation by 7), a circle with radius of 1 cubit has a circumference of 44 palms. From this it is easy to calculate the circumference of any circle of any number of cubits radius giving an answer in palms. For example, 3 cubits = 3 × 44 = 132 palms circumference. All this is done with nice whole numbers and no nasty repeating decimals.

Now you can see why the Egyptians chose to divide their royal cubit by 7—to make circular measure very simple. In the light of the above two points, it becomes apparent why the Egyptians adopted a seked of 5.5 for many of their pyramids. Because the corresponding ratio of 7:11 already contains the numeric elements of π (7 and 22) there is a direct relationship between the main elements of the architecture of the pyramid: the square (base), the triangular (side) and the circle (the perfect figure). The numbers 7 and 11 are found in other aspects of the Great Pyramid—for example, there are 7 corbels counterbalanced on each side of the Grand Gallery.

ABOVE **The pyramids of Khafre (Cheops) and Kephren, two of the pyramids on the Giza plateau. Herodotus said there were tunnels under the former but not the latter.**

The use of Φ in the Great Pyramid

Using the same illustration used to demonstrate calculating the seked (see page 117), look at the vertical triangle HEF formed by slicing into the Pyramid halfway along one face. Now we will calculate what has been called the 'Great Pyramid Triangle' with the cubit dimensions of 280 for HE (height) and 220 for FE (half of the base length of 440 cubits). By dividing both dimensions by 220 we reduce the base to unity, and the result is:

Height: 280/220 = 1.2727' (' indicates that the 2727 repeats infinitely) = $\sqrt{\Phi}$
Base: 220/220 = 1
Therefore, the hypotenuse HF^2
= $(\sqrt{\Phi})^2 + 1^2 = \Phi + 1$
Therefore, the hypotenuse HF
= $\sqrt{\Phi} + \sqrt{1}$ (by square rooting both sides)
= Φ (which is a special case for Φ)

And so, if you consider that there is a special relationship between Φ and growth, perhaps the Great Pyramid had more to do with fertility and growth than with death and the afterlife.

Herodotus' secrets

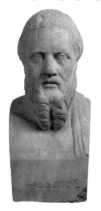

Often called the father of history, Herodotus of Halicarnassus (fifth century BC) wrote a book called Histories, *which included information about the Egyptian pyramids that he had gathered mainly from first-hand observation and discussion with Egyptian priests.*

ABOVE **Herodotus has given us the oldest and probably clearest description of the Great Pyramid as it was in the fifth century BC.**

Despite this, academics have largely disregarded Herodotus' views on the pyramids. Recently, however, they have begun to take notice because many of this ancient historian's writings about Greek and other history have been confirmed by archaeology.

So what did he say about the geometry of the pyramids? He gave the dimensions of its height as 8 plethra (which is 32.38 yards or 29.608 meters). If we convert this to a modern measure we get:

8 x 32.38 = 259.04 yards = 777.12 feet
or
8 x 29.608 = 236.864 meters

This number is far too large. But if we divide Herodotus' figure by Φ (1.6180339887…) we get exactly 480.28 feet or 146.39 meters. Now, according to the best estimates, the height of the Great Pyramid was 480.62 feet or 146.53 m, almost exactly right.

Herodotus is often criticized for gross inaccuracy, but I believe that in this case the priests had told him the absolutely correct figure, but he omitted to add that this delightful round figure of 8 had to be divided by Φ to obtain Greek *plethra*. This is possible because Herodotus was talking to the priest via a translator.

Alternatively, the Egyptians may have used the term *plethron* to indicate a unit that was Φ times smaller than the common Greek usage of the word, in which case an Egyptian *plethora* exactly equals 35 royal cubits.

Under the Great Pyramid

Herodotus reminds us that the pyramids were, in his time, still faced with polished limestone, which therefore made accurate measurements easier. He also quotes at length from what was written on the casing stones—these were sadly stripped in the Islamic era (seventh century) and taken to Cairo to build mosques.

Herodotus mentions more than once that underground chambers were hollowed out of the Giza plateau before the Great Pyramid was built. I believe the

BELOW **The head of the enigmatic Sphinx, strangely not mentioned by Herodotus, despite its age.**

Greek pyramid numerology

Isopsephy is the Greek word for numerology—the equating of letters with numbers. The practice was endemic in Greek culture. It is therefore interesting, but perhaps coincidental, that the cubit dimensions of the Great Pyramid yield some pretty interesting isopsephy. Let us take the base dimension, measured in royal cubits:

Half base = 220 = *ολον* = perfect = *οικον* = temple.

Whole base = 440 = *ο οικοσ* = the temple = *οροσ* = mountain (or limit) = *η καταβολε* = foundation = *απαντη* = everywhere.

The Egyptian word for pyramid translates as 'horizon'. So, as a speculative description of a pyramid, 'the foundation of the perfect temple mountain which stretches to the horizon (everywhere),' is not a bad interpretation.

Using the same method, the height dimension has a monotheistic ring:

Height = 280 = *σοι* = 'unto thee' = *ιοξ* = one

This is suggestive but not conclusive.

ABOVE **The King's Chamber with its strange 'sarcophagus,' which probably never held the body of Khafre (Cheops), the king who built the Great Pyramid.**

key to their location and extent is bound up in the simple Euclidean geometry that relates the Sphinx to the nearby pyramids and that it is only a matter of time before they are discovered. Herodotus makes a point of saying that there is no network of underground chambers under Kephren's pyramid (next to Khafre's pyramid).

In speaking about another pyramid Herodotus says (2:148) that "the approach to the pyramid has been built underground." This suggests that the real entrance to the Great Pyramid is probably in the underground complex, which may open some distance from the pyramid. The modern entrance is simply something that has been cut and blasted into the side of the pyramid by would-be tomb robbers and archaeologists. Even today nobody knows the location of the real entrance.

Dimensions of the Temple of Solomon

Solomon's reputation for wisdom is celebrated in Judaism, Christianity and Islam. So when he designed a temple for the Lord, we can safely assume he used the best and most sacred geometry. Fortunately, the Bible has left us with a detailed description of the temple's dimensions.

The structure of the Temple

Solomon turned to the old cultures of Phoenicia and Tyre to find the architects, masons, builders, craftsmen and even the materials he needed to build his Temple and erect a permanent sanctuary for the Ark of the Covenant.

At that time, the Temple of Melquart in Tyre was one of the most magnificent temples in the region, and it is extraordinary how closely its plan mirrors the Temple of Solomon, which therefore probably followed the traditional Phoenician design: an outer hallway

(*ulam*), a central open courtyard (*heikal*) and an inner holy of holies (*debir*).

Two large pillars stood outside the front entrance (perhaps in the style of an Egyptian-style pylon gate). They were each 35 cubits (60 feet or 18.3 meters) high and draped with 100 golden pomegranates and wreathed with ornate gold chains.

The altar for animal sacrifice in front of the temple entrance was huge: 20 cubits (34.4 feet or 10.5 meters) square and 10 cubits (17 feet or 5.2 meters) high. Also in front of the temple stood a huge brass cauldron full of water, which is translated in the King James's Version of the Bible as a 'sea.' This is usually described as a laver, or washing place, but its huge size suggests to me instead that it helped Solomon restrain the demons he was reputed to have used in the construction of the Temple. It was 10 cubits (17 feet or 5.2 meters) across, 5 cubits (8.5 feet or 2.6 meters) high and slightly over 30 cubits (51 feet or 15.6 meters) in circumference, supported on 12 outward-facing oxen made of bronze.

How big was the Temple?

The Temple was made of stone and lined with cedar panelling overlaid with gold. The innermost room, the Holy of Holies, was a cube of exactly 20 cubits (34.4 feet or 10.5 meters) and partitioned off from the main body of the Temple. It contained

BELOW An old engraving of Jerusalem showing an imaginative drawing of Solomon's Temple at the center, which bears little relation to its biblical description.

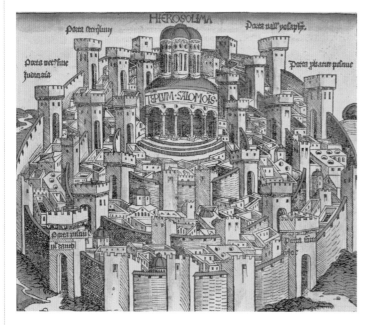

two cherubim with two pairs of wings, each 5 cubits (8.5 feet or 2.6 meters) long.

The wings touched both walls of each other's tips and therefore had a combined span of 20 cubits.

However, the dimensions of the temple itself are still a matter of debate, for if we take the biblical dimensions at face value, the Temple was quite a modest size. Yet, the second rebuilding of the Temple used truly huge stones in its foundations—these can be seen in Jerusalem today in the Wailing Wall, which is hundreds of meters long. The paved area on top, which might reasonably be expected to correspond with the ground plan of the original temple, is huge.

The mosque of the Dome of the Rock, which takes up only a small part of this area, is by itself 183.73 feet (56 m) by 183.73 feet (56 m).

The biblical dimensions are given in old cubits. Therefore, if we assume that these are the same as royal cubits (20.620 inches or 52.55 centimeters), the dimensions reveal a very small temple, but one that is astonishingly *six times higher* than it is wide:

Length = 60 old cubits
= 103.1 feet (31.4 m).
Breadth = 20 old cubits
= 34.36 feet (10.5 m).
Height = 120 cubits
= 206.2 feet (62.8 m).

These are the exact same dimensions that the Templars took back to Europe and that subsequently influenced the building of the marvellous high-ceilinged Gothic cathedrals that date from this period (see pages 132–135).

ABOVE **The Dome of the Rock mosque, built on the probable courtyard of Solomon's Temple in Jerusalem.**

I believe the only logical explanation is that the dimensions were at some stage inadvertently swapped. If so, this would make for original temple dimensions of:

Length = 120 old cubits
= 206.2 feet (62.8 m)
Breadth = 60 old cubits
= 103.1 feet (31.4 m)
Height = 20 cubits
= 34.36 feet (10.5 m)

This is a handsomely proportioned building. Notice that all the dimensions are multiples of each other and of the Holy of Holies. The numbers are right; it may just be their order that is in question. As we have seen, numbers are everything in the geometry of sacred architecture.

If we calculate the volume of the building, using these or the original figures, we get 60 x 20 x 120 = 144,000 cubic cubits. This is a significant number, as it is the number of the elect who will be saved at the end of time according to Revelations, as well as a number relating to the 12 tribes of Israel.

The Parthenon

The best-known temple of ancient Greece, the Parthenon was constructed in Athens between 447 and 438 BC to replace the old temple of Athena, which the Persians had destroyed. The new temple was built almost exclusively of marble—22 thousand tons of it.

ABOVE **The goddess Athena Parthenos, the virgin after whom the temple, the Parthenon, was named.**

The Parthenon is built on a huge platform (stylobate) and faces roughly East. This eastern face is eight columns wide and there are 17 columns along each flank. The actual temple (cella), which stands inside the columns on the stylobate, is divided into two: one is dedicated to Athena Polias and the other to Athena Parthenos (the virgin) from which the building gets its name.

The Parthenon is a sacred precinct built by some of the finest minds of the Greek culture that invented geometry, and it is therefore the archetypal example of sacred geometry applied to architecture. We know that this geometry was complex and deliberate because its architect Iktinos wrote a whole book explaining his work, which has been lost.

So it is no surprise to learn that since the end of Turkish control of Greece in 1830 many attempts have been made to deduce the mathematical rules governing the perfection of its proportions. The Golden Mean and Φ have, of course, featured in these attempts, and many books categorically state that the beauty of the dimensions of the Parthenon comes from its use of Φ, as if that was a fact. Unfortunately, it isn't. Often this 'fact' is asserted without even quoting the dimensions on which the author bases these claims; sometimes it is supported by quoting the wrong dimensions (length instead of width); and sometimes it is

supported just by drawing fanciful rectangles on oblique photographs of the Parthenon. In the most egregious case, this drawing is not even anchored by the key points of the geometry to the actual architectural features. Geometry, however, is nothing if not precise.

Front face dimensions: no Φ in sight

The actual front rectangular dimensions of the Parthenon usually quoted are 101.25 feet wide by 45.08 feet high (30.86 m by 13.7 m). Dividing one by the other we get 2.25, which is nowhere near the value of Φ (1.618 …), but it is the square of ⅔ or the ratio 9:4. We will see that 9 plays a much larger part than Φ in the dimensions of the Parthenon.

If we calculate to an estimated apex of the triangular pediment 101.25 feet wide by 58.10 feet high (30.86 m by 17.7 m), we get 1.74, closer to Φ but still not precise enough.

However, if we calculate dimensions just using the column height, 101.25 feet wide by 33.75 feet high (30.86 m by 10.286 m) we get exactly 3.0, which is a much more interesting whole number. In fact, if we look at the precise measurements (see table) we find that the sacred geometry of the Parthenon depends almost entirely on whole numbers, such as 9 and its sub-multiples, and does not need to be forced into artificial contortions to produce Φ.

ABOVE The front (and shortest side) of the Parthenon. Almost all of the inner temple and the triangular pediment above were destroyed by an explosion.

In fact, the real geometry of the front face of the Parthenon is very simple: it consists of a ratio of 3 for the columns, and $(1.5)^2 = 2.25$ for the whole rectangular face. The triangular pediment, as the Greeks well knew, is a geometric figure in its own right and should not be included in the rectangular calculations. (Ratios including this triangle are not significant, but those without it are.)

Not surprisingly, the ratio of base to height of this triangle is: $101.25/(57.60 - 44.58) = 101.25/13.02 = 7.77777…$ repeating. A fascinating number, let us put it as the Greeks would have seen it: exactly 7⅞ (not using decimals).

PARTHENON DIMENSIONS

Dimensions of Parthenon	Greek feet	Imperial feet	Meters	Greek *plethra*
Stylobate *(platform)*				
Width (eastern frontage)	*112.50*	*101.25*	*30.86*	*1.000000*
Length (depth)	*250.00*	*225.00*	*69.58*	*2.222222*
Height of columns	*37.50*	*33.75*	*10.29*	*0.333333*
Height of entablature	*12.03*	*10.83*	*3.30*	
Rectangular height (excluding triangular section)	*49.53*	*44.58*	*13.59*	
Height of triangular section	*14.47*	*3.02*	*3.97*	
Total height to apex	*64.00*	*57.60*	*17.56*	
Cella *(inner temple)*				
Width (frontage)	*77.78*	*70.00*	*21.34*	
Length (depth)	*155.56*	*140.00*	*42.6*	
Old Temple				
Old temple width	*50.00*	*45.00*	*13.72*	*0.444444*
Old temple length	*125.00*	*112.50*	*34.29*	*1.111111*

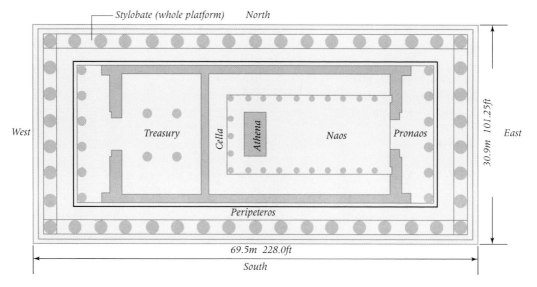

Stylobate (whole platform)   North

West   Treasury   Cella   Athena   Naos   Pronaos   East

Peripeteros

30.9m 101.25ft

69.5m 228.0ft

South

ABOVE A plan of the Parthenon showing the entrance at the east, and the structure of the inner temple (*naos*) and treasury with dimensions.

Cella dimensions

Vitruvius explains that the outer ring of columns, the *peripteros* (walkway), is simply a sort of arcade around the inner temple itself (*cella*). Essentially, the *peripteros* is a place where devotees could shelter from the frequent Mediterranean rainstorms. The front (or eastern end) of this walkway was called the *pronaos* ('in front of the *naos*'), the *naos* being the holy area of the temple itself. The dimensions of the *cella* were 140 feet long by 70 feet wide (42.67 m by 21.34 m), giving an exact ratio of 2:1.

Stylobate dimensions

The stylobate is the base of the temple. Measured at the top step, the dimensions of the Parthenon are 225 feet by 101.25 feet (68.58 m by 30.86 m). Dividing one by the other, we again get 2.2222 ... or, as the ancient Greeks would have seen it, ²⁰⁄₉.

Relationship with the old temple

I have reserved the real key to the dimensions of the Parthenon to last.

After the Persians destroyed the old temple, the architect Iktinos' remit was to build a new temple *exactly* twice the size and twice as splendid.

However, this is not as simple as it sounds. By simply doubling all dimensions you finish up with eight times the volume— not the required dimensions. Like the ancient Egptians, the ancient Greeks were very interested in the cubic measure of their buildings, and they planned to exactly double the volume of their old destroyed temple.

Doubling the cube

If s is the original side length of the old temple then its volume v is expressed as:

$$v = s^3$$

To double this volume we get:

$$2v = 2 \times s^3$$

So to get the new length n we need to calculate:

$$n = \sqrt[3]{(2 \times s^3)} = \sqrt[3]{2} \times s = 1.26 \times s$$

Therefore, to double the volume, all sides should be increased by a factor of 1.26.

The number 9

Note that the number 9 figures through-out the whole constructions, and that proportions of 9 always produce intriguing self-repeating decimals that are 'pure' numbers. For example:

⅑ = 0.111111 ...
²⁄₉ = 0.222222 ...
³⁄₉ = 0.333333 ...
⁴⁄₉ = 0.444444 ...
¹⁰⁄₉ = 1.111111 ...
²⁰⁄₉ = 2.222222 ... and so on

These all form repdigits. (A repdigit is a number consisting of a single, repeated, non-zero digit, such as 11 or 22 or 555555.) Indeed, the two measures that have been used on the Parthenon—the imperial foot and the Greek trimmed foot—relate to each other in an exact ratio of ¹⁰⁄₉ or 1.111111... .

If we use another Greek measure of distance, the *plethron*, which Herodotus used to describe the dimensions of the Great Pyramid, we get another series of repdigits (see table below).

So there you have it, the key to the sacred geometry of the Parthenon is 9, not Φ!

KEY RATIOS OF THE SACRED GEOMETRY

Greek foot to Greek trimmed foot	*1.111111'*	*10/9*
Cella width to cella length	*2.000000*	*18/9*
Length to width	*2.222222'*	*20/9*
Width to height of columns	*3.000000*	*27/9*
Length to height of columns	*6.666666'*	*60/9*

Visual tricks

One of the unique tricks of geometry incorporated into the Parthenon is a subtle deforming of the dimensions. This used to be taken as evidence of carelessness or subsidence but has now been recognized as deliberate. The corner columns are slightly larger in diameter and all columns bulge slightly as they rise, and curve outwards, in accordance with the ancient rules of perceived perspective.

The stylobate itself is not flat but has an upward curvature towards its center of 2.36 inches (60 mm) on the east and west ends and of 4.33 inches (110 mm) on the sides. This not only allows rain to run off but also has a more subtle visual effect. The distortions are deliberate and the south side, the west side and the height of the southeast corner were all 0.25 inches or ¹⁄₄₈ foot (6 mm) greater than their opposite dimension. The usual explanation for this is that the architects knew, about and wanted to compensate, for the viewer's apparent retinal curvature, which causes a slight distortion in the perception of straight lines.

ABOVE A corner column of the Parthenon. The columns were slightly bulbous to allow for the distorting effects of the human eye.

The architecture of man

Probably the most influential architectural book of all time is the Ten Books of Architecture *which were written in the first century* BC *by the Roman architect Marcus Vitruvius Pollo. In them he summarized the rules of his Roman and Greek predecessors.*

When his books were rediscovered about AD1000 they helped trigger the burst of Renaissance architectural splendour that was to produce some of the most beautiful buildings of all time, buildings designed by architects who were also great artists, such as Donato Bramante (1444–1514) and Leone Battista Alberti (1404–1472). The books codified the exact proportions of the different orders of columns—Doric, Ionic and Corinthian. This was geometric knowledge that had been lost to the world since the demise of the Roman Empire.

Vitruvian man

One of the illustrations that Leonardo da Vinci drew for Luca Pacioli's book (see pages 144–145) has always been referred to as 'Vitruvian man'. Its essence was to illustrate Vitruvius' remark that, with the hands raised above the head, a circle can be inscribed using the navel as the center and a perfect square can be formed by the man with his arms outstretched. This has attracted many interpretations and many 'interpretative' geometrical constructions involving the *vesica pisces* (see pages 130–31), pentagons, various diagonals and so on have been drawn over it in an attempt to elucidate various things. However, accurate measurement dispels many of these interpretations.

Let us look at Vitruvian man. Leonardo's circle is drawn with its center on the navel in accordance with the supposition that the navel divides man's height according to the *phi* ratio. Leonardo was nothing if not a good observer and he drew his Vitruvian man from life, but the result was a ratio of 1.656. He soon found that the geometric center of man in fact lies just above the penis and accordingly drew a circumscribing square instead. Its diagonals meet at the key point just at the base of the penis.

RIGHT A self-portrait of Leonardo da Vinci, a true Renaissance all-rounder whose discoveries were well ahead of his time, even now.

Leonardo's cubits

It seems few commentators have actually read the notes that Leonardo wrote on the same page of his notebook. If they had they would have seen that there is a scale below the picture that is annotated 'palms.' There are 6 palms divisions of one standard (non-royal) cubit. If you look at Leonardo's scale below the drawing you will see that it is in cubits. Each cubit is divided into 6 palms, and the very end palms are even divided into 4 fingers each. There is no doubt that Leonardo was using this illustration simply to experiment with cubit measures applied to the human body, not *phi*, pentagons or any other elaborate interpretations.

Now if you look at the arms directly above the cubit divider marks you will see that they are also marked, so I have drawn back in the original vertical cubit divisions from these markings. A vertical drawn from the centre of the hair parting completes the vertical division: Vitruvian man with arms outstretched is exactly 4 cubits wide. Then look carefully at the knees of the centre legs and you will see that Leonardo drew cut marks across them, as he did also at penis and nipple level. If you extend these marks, you will see that Vitruvian man divides exactly into 4 cubits height. This is precisely what Leonardo was seeking to check or prove, rather than the myriad of other more mystical speculations often suggested.

A further refinement to the drawing is the horizontal lines on the face, which embody the dictum that the face divides at the base of the nose halfway between the hairline and the breastbone. I have left the other construction lines unemphasized to show Leonardo's other construction lines.

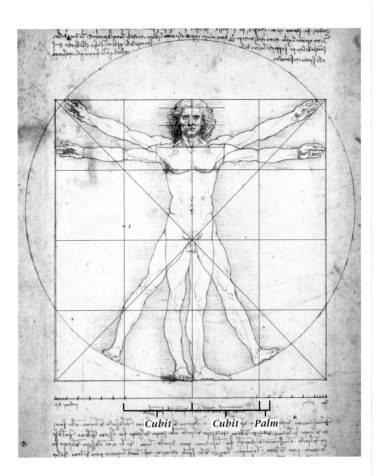

Cubit — Cubit — Palm

ABOVE Leonardo's 'Vitruvian man', whose original purpose was only to show how the cubit measure of ancient Egypt could be applied to the dimensions of man.

Eurhythmy

Vitruvius said: "When every important part of the building is thus conveniently set in proportion by the right correlation between heights and width, between width and depth, and when all these parts have also their place in the total symmetry of the building, we obtain *eurhythmy*." The Renaissance coined the term *commodulatio* to express this sound symmetry.

Christianity and the sacred feminine

The vesica piscis *(or* ichthys*) is a symbol made from two circles of the same radius, intersecting in such a way that the center of each circle lies on the circumference of the other. The Latin words literally mean the 'bladder of the fish.'*

It is said that, before Christianity, the *vesica piscis* also conveyed the meaning of 'vulva' or 'womb.' The Mother Goddess was often portrayed with pendulous breasts, heavy buttocks and a conspicuous vulva. This is the upright *vesica piscis*, which Christians later adopted and turned through 90 degrees to serve as their symbol, long before the calvary cross became their prime symbol. It is interesting that a symbol of plenty preceded a symbol of death.

Early Christians in the Roman Empire had to protect themselves by keeping their meeting places secret. In order to point the way to ever-changing meeting places, they developed the symbol of the *vesica piscis* with a tail (a fish) that they could chalk on walls in advance of a meeting and remove later.

Why choose a fish symbol?

The Greek word, *ichthys* means 'fish.' There are several hypotheses as to why the fish was chosen. One is that it refers to the biblical story in which Jesus miraculously fed 5,000 people with fish and bread. Another is that it refers to his

---

Calculating the length of the *vesica piscis*

Use the Pythagorean right-angled triangle COB and assume the radius = 1.
Hypotenuse $CB^2 = OB^2 + CO^2$
Therefore $OB^2 = CB^2 - CO^2$
$OB^2 = 1^2 - (\frac{1}{2})^2$
$OB^2 = 1 - \frac{1}{4} = 0.75$
$OB = \sqrt{0.75} = 0.8660254$
Therefore, $AB = 2 \times OB = 2 \times 0.8660254 = 1.7320508$
Which just happens to be $\sqrt{3}$.
So the length AB of the *vesica piscis* is $\sqrt{3}$.

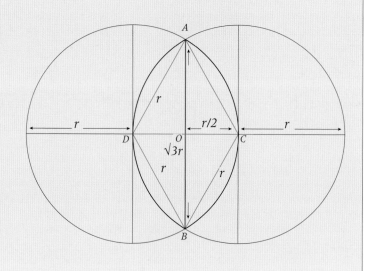

description as a 'fisher of men' or simply that it was the previous profession of some of his disciples, that of fishermen.

The isopsephy (numerical addition) of the Greek letters for fish adds to 1,219. Other Greek phrases that also add up to 1,219 include: 'The omega,' a reference to Christ as 'alpha and omega,' or the beginning and end. 'Joy and gladness' and 'The logos of the Father' also add up to this figure.

The geometry of the *vesica piscis*

The *vesica piscis* is made by drawing two circles (with centres C and D) intersecting each other (at points A and B), but the centre of one circle is on the circumference of the other and vice versa. The result of this is that the width of the *vesica piscis* (CD) is, of course, just one radius, or *r*, and two equilateral triangles (ACD and DCB) are formed.

If you draw a vertical line between the two points of circle intersection (AB) the length of the *vesica piscis* can be calculated to be $\sqrt{3}$ or 1.7320508 … .

The length:width ratio of the *vesica piscis* was expressed by Pythagoras (who considered it a sacred figure) as 153:265, a ratio sometimes known as 'the measure of the fish.' In the Bible when Jesus helps his disciples to catch fish, he catches exactly 153 fish. This ratio of 153:265 is sometimes further approximated to 15:26.

Renaissance artists frequently surrounded images of Jesus with the *vesica piscis*, and it was later also used to frame depictions of the Virgin Mary. It is sometimes seen as almond-shaped, when it is called a *mandorla* (Italian for almond). In Christian art some haloes appear in the shape of a vertical *vesica piscis*. The seals of ecclesiastical organizations are often enclosed within a *vesica piscis*, a format copied by Aleister Crowley. A more modern yet secular version is the ball used in rugby, which resembles a 3-D *vesica piscis*.

ABOVE A unicursal triquetra, a figure generated from three *vesica pisces*.

Milan Cathedral

The long drawn-out construction of Milan Cathedral saw many changes and many new plans. During the rulership of the Duke Francesco Sforza several artists worked on the building, and both Leonardo da Vinci and Bramante were kept busy working out the proportions of the dome.

The plans published in 1521 by the architect Caesar Caesariano are often quoted in works on sacred geometry, but they remained theoretical and were not in fact put into practice. The present shape of the Milan Duomo does not correspond with these plans, except in basic components, such as the number of entrance doors. Nevertheless, these plans are an insight into the methods used by the architects of the period.

Concentric circles
The first thing you notice is the triangular lines drawn from the pinnacle of the tower, which some writers have suggested indicate that the plans are an example of *ad triangulum* design (design based on the triangle). In fact, this is not the case and the front elevation of the cathedral is

based upon a series of concentric circles, spaced 14 units apart. A clue comes from the C that is marked on their center on the plan. Although Caesariano drew only three circles, it is obvious he used six circles to construct his plan, and I have taken the liberty of drawing the others in accordingly. These circles mark in turn (beginning with the smallest one):

• The width of the main door pillars based at C and D and also the height of the outer side doors.
• The ground level and centerpoint of the main door, marked Z, and the line E-bar, which marks the top of the two supporting Gothic door arches either side of the main door.
• The positions of the pillars based at B and E (radius 42).
• The positions of the pillars based at A and F, and the flat roof alignment level with G (radius 56).
• The positions of the pillars based at H and K (radius 70).
• The base of the central steeple roof marked N^1–R^1 and the ends of the main flat roof (radius 84).

The two rulers
I have drawn in the three inner circles to show the completely regular diminishing radii of construction, which in each case is exactly 14 units. I use the term 'units' as

RIGHT **Milan Cathedral today, after many changes of design.**

Caesariano marks two scales at the top of his design, but does not identify their units. The whole plan of the structure is based on these two rulers, HZ and KZ, which each have 64 divisions. These scales enable one to read off all relevant proportions and hence appreciate the harmony of the design.

Using those rulers, the proportions of the façade can be unravelled. For example, the whole width of the cathedral comes to 144 units, which is a recurring biblical number, used in Revelations for the number of souls who will be saved and for various dimensions of the New Jerusalem:

The height to top of spire = 168 = 12 x 7 x 2 units

The height to top flat roof = 84 = 12 x 7 units

The width = 144 = 12 x 12 units

The main circle diameter = 168 = 12 x 7 x 2 units

The radius between circles = 14 = 7 x 2 units

So you can see that the modulus for this cathedral is an interplay between 12 and 7, not *phi*, as every other commentator seems to remark. Also, it is the interaction between the circles, whose radius increases by 14 (= 7 x 2) at each inscription, that controls the whole geometry; the horizontal lines generated by these circles give the vertical proportions. The triangular constructions only come much later, based on the circles and horizontal lines. These are simply the means of fixing the height of the components of the spire.

The circles are all centered on point C, which is a point exactly one-third of the height of the flat roofline. The diameter of the largest circle is exactly equal to the height of the whole structure.

ABOVE The original design of Caesar Caesariano (1521), based on a series of evenly spaced concentric circles and a modulus of 12 and 7 units, the Zodiac and the 7 planets.

Chartres Cathedral

Part of the rebuilding of Chartres Cathedral was inspired by St Bernard of Clairvaux (1090–1153), one of the most influential churchmen of his time, and sometimes called "the second founder" of the Cistercian order of monks. Bernard was chosen by the pope to promote the second crusade in 1145 and was responsible for devising the rules of the Knights Templar, whose headquarters were in the ruins of Solomon's Temple in Jerusalem.

The seed from which Gothic architecture grew may have been the intense interest in the proportions of the original Temple of Solomon (see pages 122–23), which appeared to specify an extraordinarily high roof. Chartres provided the roots of inspiration and technical know-how for many of the other great Gothic cathedrals, specifically the design of the flying buttress (which is also reflected in the three storeys high rooms propping up either side of Solomon's Temple). The two towers of Chartres are of very different styles and sizes, and may reflect the Jachin and Boaz pillars of Solomon's Temple, one representing the Moon and one the Sun, as shown by the sun and moon images on their steeples.

The geometry of the flying buttresses (see illustration) had to be calculated very carefully to transfer the huge weight of the roof spans downward to the ground rather than outward, which would have destroyed the walls. This geometry is based on circles. The centers of these in this buttress cross-section fall on the same vertical line Y^1Y^2 drawn down the face of the wall. These three circle centers also correspond to the three main levels (marked H^1, H^2 and H^3).

• You can clearly see that the arch of the highest buttress arch is based on a circle centred at C^1.
• Directly below this, the circle centered at C^2 provides the arch line for the curve of the main buttress.
• Below that is a circle centered on C^3, which defines the right side of the ground-level Gothic arch.
• The left side of this arch is generated by an interlocking circle, which creates the *vesica pisces* A^1A^2 whose central line forms level H^3.
• Finally, the large internal Gothic arch to the left is formed from the *vesica pisces* V^1V^2, which is based on E^1E^2, a level set exactly halfway between H^1 and H^2.
• Many other geometric relationships and ratios link together this precisely balanced structure—for example, the height H^2 is 0.666 of the height H^1.

The Chartres labyrinth

Chartres is the only remaining cathedral with a labyrinth set in stone in its floor. The custom of putting labyrinths on church floors is very ancient—for example, a labyrinth was constructed in the church of San Vitale at Ravenna as early as the sixth century.

During the crusades that were promoted in the 11th and 12th centuries, labyrinths began to be used as a substitute pilgrimage for Jerusalem—they were even called *chemins de Jerusalem*. Christians, unable to travel to Jerusalem, would walk the labyrinths, often on their knees in penance. The paths of the Chartres labyrinth make for a journey of 261 meters (858 feet). An interesting coincidence is that the numerical value of the Greek word *muesis*, or 'initiation,' is 858.

The Chartres labyrinth is an 11-circuit labyrinth, meaning that from one edge to the center there are 11 circuits, or paths, made by 12 concentric circles. It is unicursal, which means there is only one path through it. The entire symbolism of the labyrinth was reversed by Christian usage: rather than a place to escape from (the lair of the Minotaur), the centre became the goal or spiritual Jerusalem.

The lunations surrounding the labyrinth

The outer edge of the labyrinth at Chartres is marked by a circle of crescent shapes called lunations. There are 114 lunations, of which two are only partly present to allow for the entrance. This suggests a lunar symbolism for the labyrinth, as there are 28 lunations to each quarter, and 28 x 4 = 112. The seal of the Knights Templar also featured a large crescent moon.

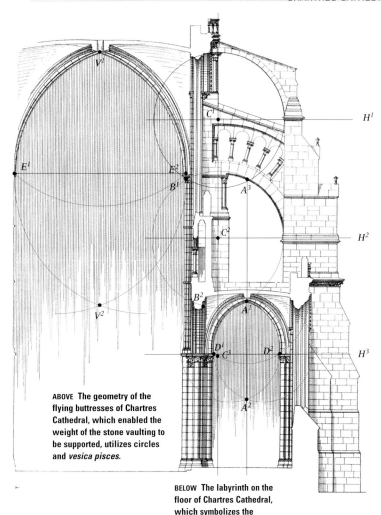

ABOVE The geometry of the flying buttresses of Chartres Cathedral, which enabled the weight of the stone vaulting to be supported, utilizes circles and *vesica pisces*.

BELOW The labyrinth on the floor of Chartres Cathedral, which symbolizes the pilgrimage to Jerusalem.

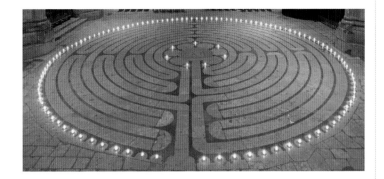

St. Paul's Cathedral

Skilled in four professions that relate to sacred geometry, Sir Christopher Wren was not only a superb architect but also an accomplished mathematician, astronomer and metrologist. He contributed to both Kepler's work on orbits and to Newton's on gravity.

ABOVE **Sir Christopher Wren, the architect of St. Paul's and many other churches in the City of London, was also a skilled astronomer, polymath and metrologist.**

After the Great Fire of London in 1666 Wren helped to replan the entire city of London and supervised the rebuilding of no fewer than 51 churches. In 1657 he became Professor of Astronomy at Gresham College, London, and was Savilian Professor of Astronomy at Oxford between 1661 and 1673. It was after this appointment that he made his most important contributions to mathematics.

Sir Isaac Newton, never one to give excessive praise to others, states in his *Principia* that he ranks Wren together with John Wallis (1616–1703), an English geometer, cryptographer and mathematician, and Christiaan Huygens (1629–1695), a Dutch mathematician and astronomer who did much work on time-keeping, optics and calculus—as the leading mathematicians of the day.

Wren's fame in mathematics also stems from results he obtained in 1658 when he found the length of an arc of the cycloid (see pages 50–51), using a proof based on dissections to reduce the problem to summing segments of the chords of a circle that are in geometric progression.

Wren was the first to resolve the problem set by Kepler, in which a semi-circle is cut with a line in a given ratio through a given point on its diameter. This problem was very real one, for it had arisen from Kepler's work on elliptical orbits (see pages 78–79). Kepler reduced the problem of finding the mean motion of a planet to that of cutting an ellipse in a given ratio with a line through the ellipse focus.

Wren independently proved Kepler's third law, which links the period it takes for a planet to circle the Sun with its distance from the Sun. This law proves Pythagoras' contention that there is a 'music of the spheres,' or, to put it less poetically, definite mathematical relationships between the orbits and the period of revolution of the planets.

RIGHT **The interior of St. Paul's Cathedral showing the 365 foot (111 m) dome and almost Solomonic pillars before the altar.**

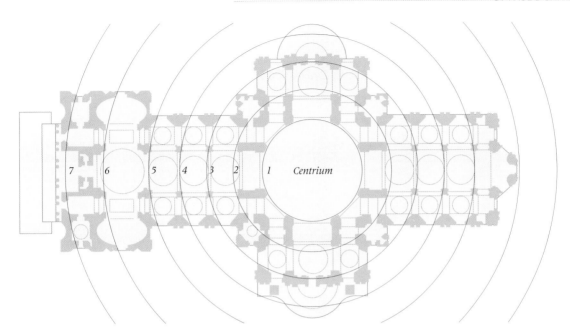

7 6 5 4 3 2 1 *Centrium*

Wren was also very much into measurement and was involved in metrology, the science of standardized measurement. In fact, it was he who first proposed in England that the basic unit of length measurement should be derived from time, specifically the length of a pendulum with exactly a one-second swing (see page 87).

St. Paul's Cathedral

Wren's ground plan for St. Paul's Cathedral is a prime example of sacred geometry. The length of the building is 'all fiveness' at 555 feet (169.16 m), including the impressive entrance steps. This is coincidentally the same as the height of the Washington Memorial, which reputedly has Masonic connections, too. The length is 6,660 inches, definitely a number with inbuilt solar and apocalyptic (the number of the Beast) symbolism.

The use of key numbers does not stop with the plan. The cathedral is built of Portland stone in a late Renaissance style. Its impressive dome (inspired by St. Peter's Basilica in Rome) rises 365 feet (111 m) to the cross at its summit, marking one foot for each day of the year. Wren placed the main entrance in the west so that the congregation could face the high altar located in the east.

Wren's underlying structure is visible. The building is constructed on a base of concentric circles. The key is to be found in each of the 25 or 29 open spaces in the cathedral where he has inscribed a circle. From the large circle in the center of the cathedral it is possible to mark off seven circles radiating outwards (reminiscent of the Earth plus seven planets, or seven heavens). Each circle touches the curved inner edge of the pillars of each bay. To make the point even more obvious, these pillars are curved to fit his generating circles. The rectangular entrance steps at the western end of the cathedral are outside the circular design.

Modern organic architecture

Some modern architects have created a kind of fluid architecture that rejects the Euclidean geometry of classical building and embraces organic and flowing forms. By bringing the curves of nature back into buildings they have reawakened the idea that a building can echo archetypal shapes rather than just being a cubic accommodation box.

This desire to use the sacred geometry of nature in building is both aesthetically gratifying and a realization that it is not just temples that deserve this treatment. With the detailed study of the underlying mathematics of nature's forms, the use of non-linear geometry and computer modelling, architects are now able to explore an exciting and little-known world of non-linear organic structures. Nature is now viewed as being a mercurial mixture of both order and chaos, pattern and accident, simplicity and complexity. It is not surprising that this has inspired new concepts. Perhaps Richard Buckminster Fuller (1895–1983) is the best known of these architects with his strictly geometrically geodesic domes, but the movement goes back to the late 19th century.

Antonio Gaudí

Probably the first architect to anticipate the surrealists and achieve this on a grand scale was the Spanish architect Antonio Gaudí (1852–1926). Gaudí closely observed natural forms and was a bold structural innovator. He used geometric models made of string and weights to predict the catenary (chain) shape and stresses of his structures. He designed balanced structures that needed no internal bracing or external buttressing, as the Gothic cathedrals did. He achieved this by using catenary, hyperbolic and parabolic curves for his arches and vaults, supported by inclined columns and helicoidal (spiral cone) piers.

His greatest work, the cathedral of the Sagrada Familia in Barcelona, is yet to be completed. It is probably true to say that no cathedral will ever be built like it again. Gaudí designed many other structures— apartment blocks that were covered in melting, organic, art nouveau shapes (some with a strange mix of Catalan and Masonic symbolism), weird pinnacled lodges, serpentine mosaic benches, and winding rustic viaducts. To find equivalent rounded forms you have to go back thousands of years to the strange curved megalithic temples dedicated to the Mother Goddess on Malta.

Rudolf Steiner

Another strand of the organic tradition had its roots in German culture. The Austrian occultist Rudolf Steiner (1861–1925) was so impressed with the studies of Johann Wolfgang von Goethe into morphology and the metamorphosis

BELOW Antonio Gaudís organically structured cathedral The Sagrada Familia, Barcelona, which utilized natural forms in an art nouveau context.

of plants and animals that he referred to Goethe as 'the Galileo of the organic.'

He also applied Goethe's ideas of metamorphosis to art and architecture, copying the dynamics of form visible in all living organisms, whereby an orderly and cyclic transformation can be traced from seed to calyx to blossom to fruit (and back to seed again). These, together with Goethe's theory of color, had a deep impact on Steiner's later life and his anthroposophic architectural theories. His two Goetheanums were dramatic buildings illustrative of this new style. Such architecture has now grown into an international 'organic' movement, with examples in Europe, USA and Australia.

Modern London

London has generated a large number of organically inspired buildings in the last few decades. Some, such as the Millennium Dome designed by Sir Richard Rogers, have been expensive and flamboyant failures. More successful curvilinear shapes include the bulbous and pompous London mayoral headquarters (designed by Sir Norman Foster), which stares at London Bridge like an indignant eye, and the sleekly surreal Media Centre at Lord's Cricket Ground (designed by Future Systems, which used boat builders to fabricate the precision parts in order to get the curves right).

Sydney Opera House

The huge and controversial concrete and ceramic roof of the Sydney Opera House, which was designed originally by Danish architect Jorn Utzon, echoes the natural shells of the nearby sea but also the essence of a complex structural and

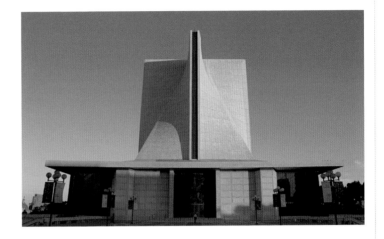

geometric problem. The saga of this construction is well known—many compromises had to be made to the original design, but the organic curves of the original concept still show clearly.

St. Mary's Cathedral, San Francisco

Paul Ryan's design for St. Mary's Cathedral in San Francisco utilizes a hyperbolic paraboloid for the shape of its 200 foot (61 m) high roof. This piece of geometry had not been discovered during the days of the great Gothic cathedrals—perhaps such computer-generated designs are part of the future of sacred geometry.

ABOVE **St. Mary's Cathedral in San Francisco, which has the distinction of having its roof designed around a hyperbolic paraboloid, a completely new geometric shape.**

BELOW **Sydney Opera House inspired by the organic curves of sea shells and the geometry of wind-blown sails.**

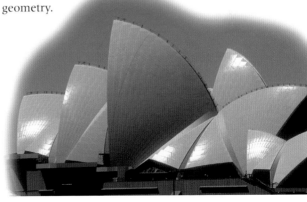

CHAPTER 7

SACRED GEOMETRY IN ART

During the Renaissance the same individuals were often responsible for constructing buildings and paintings, which meant that the tradition of sacred geometry was reflected in both art and architecture. Early experiments in optics by Roger Bacon (and later by Leonardo and Albrecht Dürer) generated rules of perspective that released artists from the flat 2-D painting of the Middle Ages. At the same time, Greek and Roman architectural ideas, with their associated sacred geometry, fuelled the building boom of the Renaissance.

Perspective created a new field of projective geometry, which enabled map-makers to capture the spherical nature of the Earth's surface on flat surfaces. The maps, in turn, enabled explorers and sailors to explore the world, creating colonial empires in a way that would not otherwise have been possible.

We look at how paintings such as Leonardo's *Last Supper* used the geometry of perspective and also incorporated symbolic numbers (in this case 13 perspectival rays for Christ and his 12 disciples). We also look at how the perfect circle in Poussin's *Les Bergers d'Arcadie* encompasses the main figures whose staves create a pair of pentagrams, framing the cryptic motto that inspired several recent best-selling expositions.

Roger Bacon: geometry, light and optics

Perhaps the earliest text that relates to perspective in art is Euclid's book on Optics, *but it was the Arab mathematician and physicist al-Haytham or Alhazen (965–1039) who gave the first correct explanation of vision, showing that light is reflected from an object into the eye.*

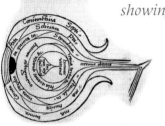

ABOVE Bacon dissected the eyeball to determine how light rays are translated into ocular vision.

Al-Haytham studied the complete science of vision, called *perspectiva* in mediaeval times. He did not apply his ideas to painting, but Renaissance artists later made important use of his optics. Roger Bacon (*c.*1214–1294) saw that geometry could be applied to optics and, as if to justify his interest, affirmed that mathematics "has always been used by all the saints and sages more than all other science." He thought mathematics could be unlocked by what he called the "flower of the whole of philosophy." This was the science of light, later to be called optics. Bacon correctly thought that all objects gave off rays of reflected light and that the eye was a receptor of images, rather than a sender of images as had previously been thought by medieval theologians. Bacon discovered, after dissecting animal eyes, that rays of light fell perpendicularly on the eyeball, carrying the image with them to receptors at the back of the eye.

Unlocking secrets

Both Bacon and Robert Grosseteste (*c.*1175–1253), his philosophical sparring partner at the University of Paris, embraced the concept of mathematics as the hidden language of nature. They hoped their quest to make science more analytical and experimental would lead to the uncovering of the exact relationships between nature and mathematics via geometry. With the geometry of light (optics and perspective) they thought they had found the study that would unlock some of the major secrets of the universe.

Bacon believed that geometry could give him access to the archetypal forms behind creation generated by the mind of the creator, and that of these, light (with its parallel Euclidean rays) was the purest expression, and, for him, that was no mere metaphor. According to Genesis (1:3–4): "And God said, Let there be Light: and there was light. And God saw the light, that it was good: and God divided the light from the darkness."

Light for Bacon was 'God in operation,' the visible manifestation of God's spiritual power, for had not God made light before anything else in the universe, and confirmed that it was indeed good? Bacon was searching for literal enlightenment.

This kind of hands-on approach earned Bacon the reputation of being the first modern scientist, and when Dr John Dee (see pages 93–95) was engaged on research into Euclid's *Elements*, and optics in particular, he looked back to Roger Bacon's work. The fact that Bacon had also made forays into magic made him the ideal mentor for Dee's skrying with crystals, as this was for Dee the bridge between the angels, optics and magic.

Geometric perspective in the service of painting

The geometry of perspective was a necessary prerequisite for the production of great art and great architecture. It was not until perspectiva *passed into the hands of artists that it was applied at a practical level rather than being purely an object of research.*

ABOVE Filippo Brunelleschi, the formulator of the basic rules of perspective and the discoverer of the vanishing point so successfully used in Renaissance paintings.

Artists have always had a pressing need to present 3-D reality on a flat canvas. Early medieval artists confined themselves to portraiture, or framed and throned saints and Madonnas, with perhaps a few angels or demons hovering nearby. Of course, these were not a problem as angels or demons did not need to fit into the perspective because they were from another dimension.

Early perspectival attempts consisted of placing foreground objects partly in front of distant ones, but the concept that size diminishes at a distance did not impinge, with the result that there were huge distortions of size and distance.

By the 13th century Giotto (*c.*1266–1337) was painting scenes that created the impression of depth by using a few simple rules. He inclined lines above eye-level he downwards, while lines below eye-level were inclined upwards, as they appeared to move away from the viewer. Similarly, lines to the left or right were inclined towards the center. Although it was not a precise mathematical formu-lation, Giotto managed by this technique to represent depth on a flat surface.

Vanishing point

The person who is credited with the first real formulation of linear perspective (*c.*1413) is Filippo Brunelleschi (1377–1446). He invented the idea of a single vanishing point, or focus, to which all parallel lines in the picture should converge. He also devised an exact calculation for the relationship between the actual length of an object and its 'visual length' in the picture, which depended on its distance from the viewer. Using these mathematical principles, he drew two demonstration pictures of buildings in Florence on wooden panels incorporating correct perspective. One was of the octagonal baptistery of St. John.

Then he came up with a brilliant idea to prove the accuracy of his theory. He bored a small hole in the painting of St. John's at precisely the vanishing point. A spectator was then asked to look through the hole from behind the panel at a mirror that reflected the panel.

In this way Brunelleschi controlled precisely the positioning of the spectator's eye so that the geometry of the vanishing point was guaranteed to be correct. Unfortunately, these paintings by Brunelleschi have been lost. The great Italian architect Leon Alberti (1404–1472) wrote an explanation of how the rules of perspective work in his treatise *On Painting*, which he dedicated to Brunelleschi.

The most mathematical of all the works on perspective written by Italian Renaissance artists was by Piero della Francesca (*c.*1420–1492). Piero was one of the leading artists of the period, and he was also the leading mathematician. In *Trattato d'abaco* Piero included material on arithmetic, algebra and geometry. He illustrated the text with diagrams of solid figures drawn in perspective.

Piero della Francesca's works were in turn heavily relied on by Luca Pacioli for his own books (see pages 144–145). Pacioli, developed exact formulae to find the relationship between the distance from the eye to the object, and its size on the canvas.

Light and shade

Around 1500 the German artist Albrecht Dürer (1471–1528) took perspective geometry back to Germany after learning as much as he could from mathematicians such as Pacioli. In 1525 he published a book that contained his theory of shadows and perspective. Geometrically, his theory is similar to that of Piero, but he stressed the importance of light and shade in depicting correct perspective. His book also described various mechanical aids that could be used to draw images in correct perspective (see illustration above).

TOP **Dürer's perspective machine being used to create a drawing with true perspective. The artist's angle of view and eye must remain fixed at the tip of the obelisk.**

ABOVE **William Hogarth's mockery of a perspective-less drawing, showing far distant things integrating with much closer objects.**

Luca Pacioli and Divine Proportion

The classic text of Renaissance geometric proportion was Luca Pacioli's De divina proportione. *Illustrated by none other than Leonardo da Vinci and published in 1509, it was extremely influential.*

Luca Pacioli (*c*.1445–1517) lived as a child in Sansepolcro, Italy, where he received part of his education in the studio of the artist Piero della Francesca, who was no stranger to elegant proportion. Pacioli's writings were strongly influenced by Piero.

Pacioli moved to Venice where he certainly seemed to know all the right people, for when he left Venice and travelled to Rome, he spent several months living with Leon Battista Alberti, one of the greatest Renaissance artists and architects and an excellent scholar and mathematician.

Some time during the next few years, Pacioli became a Franciscan friar, which is why he is dressed in monk's robes in the famous portrait by Jacopo de' Barbari (see below left). In this picture he is using a glass, water-filled, Platonic solid in his lecture. The slightly effeminate student beside him has not been identified, but might even be a young Leonardo.

While Pacioli was teaching at the University of Perugia from 1477 to 1480 he wrote a work on arithmetic for his pupils. In 1489, after two years in Rome, Pacioli returned to Sansepolcro and worked on his second most famous book, *Summa de arithmetica, geometria, proportioni et proportionalita*. This contained material on arithmetic, algebra, geometry, and trigonometry and was to provide a basis for the major progress in mathematics that was about to take place in Europe. It featured many thinkers important to sacred geometry, including Euclid, Sacrobosco and Fibonacci.

The Duke of Milan's court

In 1494 Ludovico Sforza (1452–1508), the second son of Francesco Sforza, assumed the title of Duke of Milan. Showing generous patronage to many artists and scholars, he set about making his court in Milan the finest in the whole of Europe. Leonardo da Vinci had entered Ludovico's service as a court painter and engineer in 1482; around 1496 Luca Pacioli was invited to teach mathematics. Pacioli and Leonardo quickly became close friends, and they undoubtedly discussed mathematics and art at length.

BELOW Luca Pacioli, in monk's robes, lecturing. In the foreground and suspended by a string is a glass model of one of Plato's perfect solids.

At this time Pacioli began his most famous work, *De divina proportione*, and few mathematicians can have had a more talented illustrator for their book! The book focused on the Divine Proportion that was so important in art and architectural design and on Euclid's theorems that relate to this ratio. It also explored regular and semi-regular polygons (see page 54).

Pacioli and Leonardo fled together to Florence in December 1499, three months after the French captured Milan. Pacioli was appointed to teach geometry at the University of Pisa in Florence in 1500, where he remained, teaching geometry,

until 1506. During his time in Florence, Pacioli was involved with Church affairs as well as with mathematics. He was elected the superior of his order in Romagna, and, in 1506, he entered the monastery of Santa Croce in Florence. In 1509, he published his three-volume work *De divina proportione*, and also a Latin translation of Euclid's *Elements*. Some of Pacioli's critics have claimed that he took many of his ideas on proportion from Piero della Francesca. Despite the lack of originality in Pacioli's work, his contributions to mathematics and the influence of his books are very important.

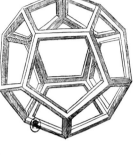

ABOVE One of Leonardo's 3-D illustrations of a Platonic solid for Pacioli's book on divine proportion.

BELOW The façade of the Monastery of Santa Croce where Pacioli worked on *De divina proportione*.

Leonardo's use of perspective

Leonardo da Vinci wrote in 1505 that "proportion is found not only in numbers and measurements but also in sounds, weights, time, positions, and in whatsoever powers there may be." But proportion was of no use if the perspective was not correct.

Perspective machines (perspectographs) were invented—probably by Leonardo—to help an artist view a scene through a wire grid while keeping his head unmoved at a fixed point. The artist draws the squares formed by the grid on to the canvas and attempts to draw inside each square just exactly what he sees, no matter how much it might appear foreshortened and distorted. Albrecht Dürer illustrated two such machines, suggesting that he himself used them in his drawing.

Projective geometry grew out of these experiments. It was a branch of geometry that still relied heavily on Euclid but dealt with the problems of perspective, the point of projection, parallel converging lines (a concept that would have been anathema to Euclid because it contradicted one of his postulates) and the vanishing point (see pages 142–143). It also opened the way for the geometry that, in the late 1500s, allowed Mercator and other map-makers to draw convincing, usable maps of a round Earth projected on to flat paper. Dr John Dee (see pages 93–95) had considerable practical input with the map-makers because of his experience of translating Euclid into English and his knowledge of Roger Bacon's work on optics (see page 141).

The Last Supper

As a result of these experiments, artists began to collect together the rules of perspective. Foremost among these rules was the idea of vanishing point. This was defined as the point were all the rays of light converge, or as we might express it today, the picture's (and therefore the artist's) focus. Enthusiastic exponents drew quite precise converging lines before beginning their painting, and this shows up startlingly in Leonardo da Vinci's *Last Supper*, where the lines of the ceiling, walls and windows converge dramatically on a point on Christ's head. In fact, there are 13 such radiating perspective lines, one for each of the disciples and one for Christ. Even the lines on the tiled floor under the table contribute to this effect.

To accentuate the perspective still further, Leonardo made one of the

BELOW A less successful perspective machine where coordinates of points on the subject (a lute) were plotted on to the drawing using a string and pulley.

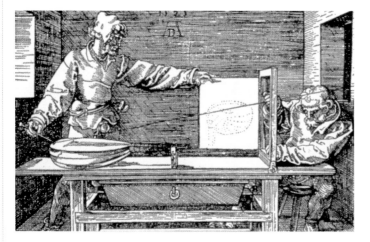

disciples, John, lean away from him. This has, of course, caused commentators to read all sorts of other significance into this rather extreme leftwards lean. It may have been done for dramatic and perspectival effect, but I don't think you can rule out the possibility that Leonardo was also making some kind of pointed reference. I don't feel that the Dan Brown's interpretation in *The Da Vinci Code* is necessarily the right one though.

I think it more likely that the extreme parting of these two figures is probably Leonardo's revenge for the continual interference in the composition of the figures at the table by the monks for whose refectory he was doing the mural. John's effeminacy and reputed homosexuality possibly prompted the monks to insist that he did not sit too close to the Master in case the picture provoked sniggers. Leonardo, in a typical

reaction that was to mark his relationship with some of his other patrons, made John's lean and effeminacy so extreme to mock the interfering monks.

Although much has been made of the groupings of the disciples, you can clearly see if you draw back from the painting and look at the arches, that Leonardo has divided his disciples into four groups of three, in each case drawing them away from the structural pillars running down from the arches supported above (see dotted lines above). This may have been done for aesthetic reasons, but it is likely it was to ensure the future integrity of the surface upon which he was painting.

Other artists caught on to perspective, but some, such as the Dutch and Flemish artists with their chess-board tiled floors, carried it to extremes, and as a result, it became an exercise in its own right rather than just a supporting structure.

ABOVE **A copy of Leonardo da Vinci's *Last Supper* after restoration showing the 13 vanishing point lines focused on Christ's head, and marked by architectural features, such as floor tiles, roof beams and window lines.**

Paintings analyzed geometrically

There have been various attempts to discover the underlying geometry of paintings. Many paintings do not have an underlying structure, except perhaps for their natural perspective, but those that do often reveal a fascinating geometry. There are four ways of doing this analysis.

Original geometric ground

The most relevant are those constructions that actually reflect the original geometric ground plan used by the artist. These are the most successful analyses, in that they reveal his original intention and are in no sense the constructions of the observer. It is sometimes even possible to see the original construction lines underneath the paint. For example, in the portrayal of Christ the Geometer the artist's original intentions are not only perfectly clear, but many traces of his original silverpoint construction lines are also still apparent.

RIGHT Five circles have been used by the artist as the underlying structure of this manuscript illumination from a Bible showing Christ as Geometer. Traces of this construction can still be seen.

Perspectival lines

The second type is a construction based on easily identifiable perspectival lines ending at a vanishing point. Such self-conscious perspectival lines occur when the vanishing point of a painting is easily identifiable and converging straight lines can be drawn on it with great certainty, usually along lines of actual architectural alignments shown in the painting.

Such constructions are not purely imaginative but were most certainly part of the artist's original planning. In fact, the exact lining up of objects along lines running to a precise vanishing point does not really occur in nature.

Two classical examples of this type of construction are Leonardo's *Last Supper* (see pages 146–147) and Piero della Francesca's *The Flagellation of Christ* (see opposite). In both cases, many vanishing point lines can be confidently drawn in.

Composition

The third type of construction is what artists usually mean when they talk of the 'composition' of a painting. Such composition depends on the relationship between the main elements of the painting or of the figures in it. It is not necessarily dependent upon straight rulings and may be neither strictly geometric nor rigidly perspectival, but nevertheless part of the conscious compositional planning of the artist.

An example of this type of painting is Nicolas Poussin's *Les Bergers d'Arcadie* (see page 151). There are definite alignments along the shepherd's staffs, and the figures are consciously grouped, but the analysis will not stand any of the complex constructions sometimes applied to this particular painting—they can also shade into the next category.

Linking vertices

The last type of geometric construction is one that imaginatively links up all possible vertices or, in many cases, points in the picture that are not even vertices. These are characterized by a mass of lines connecting everything that *might* be geometrically relevant. This procedure often produces alignments that the original artist never even considered. Worse, such a mass of lines can often obscure a simple and elegant construction. In some ways this fourth type of construction has more in common with a Rorschach inkblot test than geometry, sacred or otherwise.

Unfortunately, such geometric analyses are common, and often persist as illustrations from one book of the geometry of art to another. For example, in Dr. Funck-Hellet's treatment of Leonardo's *Leda and the Swan* he anchors his constructions on the picture frame, rather than on any of the main foci of the painting. He has added extra dotted lines at some keys points, where his main constructions miss the mark, while the major intersections of his construction lines simply focus on empty space and are devoid of any thematic significance.

In fact, in this picture, Leonardo was simply experimenting with one focal point exterior to, and to the right of, the painting. Lines drawn from that focal point faithfully trace significant alignments, such as the swan's neck, Leda's arm and head, or her right arm, or pubic mound. I have added three concentric arcs centered on exactly the same off-canvas focus, which further demonstrate that Leonardo also aligned the curve of her body, Leda's legs and thighs, with the focus of these arcs. Thus, we can see that a single point is the focus of this painting and that greatness is often derived from simplicity and elegance, rather than from a mass of overly contrived rulings.

ABOVE *The Flagellation of Christ* painted using a strict set of perspectival lines.

BELOW Leonardo da Vinci experimented with a single focal point outside the frame of the picture in *Leda and the Swan*.

The treasure of Rennes-le-Château

ABOVE **The Magdala Tower, built by the real priest Berenger Saunière in Rennes-le-Château, France, to house his private library.**

Rennes-le-Château is a sleepy provincial village at the foot of the Pyrenees in the south of France. Significantly, it lies 25 miles (40 km) from Carcassonne, which was once a stronghold of the heretical Albigensians, who were reputed to have hidden a huge treasure nearby.

The village was made famous by the extraordinary behavior of its late 19th-century priest Berenger Saunière, whose life was investigated by Michael Baigent's bestseller *The Holy Blood and the Holy Grail,* co-authored with Richard Leigh and Henry Lincoln. This fascinating book suggests that in the 1890s the priest uncovered either a literal treasure or, more likely, some hidden cipher manuscripts within the Visigothic altar pillars of his small village church, and for which he may have been paid a fabulous price.

Whatever the source, he spent a lot of money on remodelling the church, which he supplied with an extraordinary font statue of the demon Asmodeus. He built a mysterious castellated Magdala Tower to use as his library, and a zoo, an orangery and a country house (the Villa Bethania) for his mistress/housekeeper and himself.

The shadowy organization

The story unfolds to embrace the literal blood descendants of Jesus Christ and Mary Magdalene, who allegedly fled from Jerusalem to southern France, where their successors became the early Merovingian kings of France. The secret society, known as the Priory of Sion (*Pieure de Sion*), was, over the course of centuries, sworn to protect the secret. The Priory, in turn, had connections with the Templars, Godfroi de Bouillon, Baudouin IV, the leper King of Jerusalem, the Dome of the Rock and

several well-known 19th-century writers and artists.

The story spans 2,000 years and proposes that the genetic descendants of Jesus are the literal Grail Chalice that holds the Holy Blood. The Priory and its mission survived, and to come full circle, it is supposed that the priest Saunière, with his obscure references to Mary Magdalene and Asmodeus, was handsomely paid off to suppress this story.

This fabulous story became more intriguing when Dan Brown reset it into the even more fictional and even better-selling *The Da Vinci Code*. The name of the priest Saunière is re-used for the curator of the Louvre and the real organization Opus Dei is pitted against the rather more shadowy Priory of Sion.

A number of well-known artists and scientists appear on the claimed list of Grand Masters of the Priory of Sion: Nicholas Flamel, Leonardo da Vinci, Robert Fludd, Robert Boyle, Isaac Newton, Victor Hugo, Nicolas Poussin, Claude Debussy, and Jean Cocteau. As the list reaches modern times it begins to read like a "favorite famous Frenchman list" rather than a serious list of secret international Grand Masters. It begins to sound as if the later days of this shadowy organization might have simply been the invention of its alleged Grand Master, Pierre Plantard (1920–2000). Indeed, several modern researchers convincingly

LEFT Nicolas Poussin's second version of *Les Bergers d'Arcadie*, whose structure is based on one circle with a centre conveniently pointed to by the two shepherds. Their staffs form the sides of two pentagrams.

argue that the Priory of Sion is a modern hoax, the creation of Pierre Plantard and his associates, who hijacked the genuine mystery of the priest of Rennes-le-Château.

The mysterious painting

What has all that got to do with sacred geometry? The geometric key is the painting by Nicolas Poussins *Les Bergers d'Arcadie*, which is a typically idyllic scene supposedly located near Rennes-le-Château. Poussin painted two versions between 1637 and 1642, both showing three youths and a girl, perhaps shepherds, standing around an antique tomb inscribed *Et in Arcadia ego* (And in Arcadia I [am]). King Louis XIV bought the second painting (painted 1637–1638) and apparently attributed special value to it.

In Britain in 1974 a BBC 2 *Chronicle* documentary entitled *The Priest, The Painter and The Devil* featured a detailed analysis of Poussin's *Les Bergers d'Arcadie* (second version, which is displayed in the Louvre, Paris) by Professor Christopher Cornford. Formerly of the Royal College of Art, Cornford suggested that the painting was based upon pentagonal geometry (which relates to the Golden Mean). Although it is easy to draw many meaningless lines on any complex painting, this particular painting is clearly based on two circles and does not lend itself to that kind of construction.

Unfortunately, the tomb the researchers identified from the painting, found near Rennes-le-Château, has subsequently been destroyed. Also, the geometry transposed from the painting to the surrounding landscape does not really work, unless you are prepared to accept very large approximations.

Conclusion

Pythagoras said that whole numbers have a reality beyond their utility as counting sticks. He saw them as noumenal, *or the form (or ideal) behind physical reality, and maintained that they had a hand in the creation of the physical or* phenomenal *world. He thought that proportion, number and harmony were necessary to bring to fruition this beautiful universe, about which we still know relatively little.*

Without using a cyclotron, Pythagoras knew that the basic atoms (and their electron shells) must subscribe to a regular, simple and whole number arithmetic—which they do. He would not have been surprised that the universe contained just 81 stable elements, and he would have immediately recognized that number as the perfect 9 squared.

Part of the answer to the question "Why is this geometry sacred?" lies in the chapter about the logarithmic spiral (see pages 48–51), exemplified in the shape of the nautilus shell. This particular piece of geometry—*phi* and the Golden Mean— is delightfully self-replicating. The ancient Greeks, or at least Plato, would have seen the eternal shape of the nautilus as laid down in the noumenal realm, while the physical construction of the shell simply follows this blueprint. In fact, self-replication is the simplest way to design anything from cell to shell—even the construction of the universe.

I suspect that our inability to fully apprehend the universe comes from not being able to see these simple numeric patterns. As Newton, Einstein and their successors were painfully aware, the laws governing the universe are *simple*. You might expect that the formula connecting

mass to energy might cover a whole blackboard with algebraic gobble-de-gook. But what could be simpler than the elegant formula $e = mc^2$? Pythagoras might yet have the last laugh, if it is ever discovered that nothing more complex than the ten numbers of the *tetractys* governs the structure of the universe.

After all, if a falling apple can stimulate Newton to formulate the laws of gravity, why shouldn't the harmonious sound of plucked strings lead to the discovery of a unified field theory?

Bibliography

Abu-Asiya, Dawud, *Platonic and Archimedean Solids*, Wooden, Wales, 1998.

Alcock, Susan E., and Osborne, Robin, *Placing the Gods: Sanctuaries and Sacred Space in Greece*, Clarendon Press, Oxford, 1994.

Ashmore, Wendy and Knapp, A. Bernard, *Archaeologies of Landscape*, Blackwell, Oxford, 1999.

Aubrey, John, *Monumenta Britannica*, Dorset Publishing, Milborne, 1980–2.

Baigent, Michael, Leigh, Richard & Lincoln, Henry, *The Holy Blood and the Holy Grail*, Doubleday, London, 2003.

Ball, Philip, *H2O A Biography of Water*, Phoenix, London, 2002.

Bartholomew, Alick, *Crop Circles—Harbingers of World Change*, Gateway, London, 1991.

Behrend, Michael, *The Landscape Geometry of Southern Britain*, IGR, Cambridge, 1976.

Bord, Janet and Colin, *Mysterious Britain*, Paladin, 1977.

Brown, Frank, *Roman Architecture*, Studio Vista, London, 1968.

Brown, Peter, *Megaliths Myths and Men: an introduction to Astro-archaeology*, Dover, 2000.

Carmichael, David L., *Sacred Sites, Sacred Places*, Routledge, London, 1994.

Cook, Theodore Andrea, *The Curves of Life*, Dover, New York, 1979.

Cope, Julian, *The Modern Antiquarian*, Thorsons, London, 1998.

Critchlow, Keith, *Order In Space—A Design Sourcebook*, Thames & Hudson, London, 1969.

Dedron, P. and Itard, J., *Mathematics and Mathematicians Volume 1*, Transworld, London, 1973.

Dedron, P. and Itard, J., *Mathematics and Mathematicians Volume 2*, Transworld, London, 1973.

Devereux, Paul and Thomson, Ian, *The Ley Hunter's Companion*, Thames & Hudson, London, 1979.

Euclid, *Elements*, Books I–XIII, edited by Sir Thomas Heath, Dover, Mineola, 1956.

Fisher, Adrian and Kingham, Diana, *Mazes*, Shire, Buckinghamshire, 2000.

French, Peter, *John Dee: the World of an Elizabethan Magus*, RKP, London, 1972.

Ghyka, Matila, *The Geometry of Art and Life*, Dover Publications, Inc., New York, 1977.

Giorgi, Francesco, *Harmonia mundi*, Venice, 1525

Gleick, James, *Chaos*, Vintage, London, 1998.

Hawkes, Jacquetta, *Atlas of Ancient Archaeology*, Heinemann, 1974.

Hawkins, Dr Gerald, *Stonehenge Decoded*, New York, Doubleday, 1965.

Heinsch, Dr J., *Principles of Prehistoric Sacred Geography*, Zodiac House, Cambridge, 1975.

Hitching, Francis, *Earth Magic*, Cassell, London, 1976.

Holden, Alan, *Shapes, Space and Symmetry*, Columbia University Press, 1971.

Huntley, H. E., *The Divine Proportion*, Dover, New York, 1970.

Kepler, Johannes, *The Harmony of the World*, Linz, 1619.

Knight, Christopher and Butler, Alan, *Civilization One*, Watkins, London, 2004.

Lawler, Robert, *Sacred Geometry Philosophy and Practice*, Thames & Hudson, London, 1982.

Livio, Mario, *The Golden Section: the Story of Phi*, Broadway Books, New York, 2002.

Lockyer, Sir Norman. *The Dawn of Astronomy*, Kessinger, Whitefish, 1997.

McKenna, Terence and Dennis, *The Invisible Landscape*, Harper Collins, San Francisco, 1993.

Michell, John, *City of Revelation*, Garnstone, London, 1972.

Michell, John, *Ancient Metrology*, Pentacle, Bristol, 1981.

Michell, John, *The New View Over Atlantis*, Thames & Hudson, London, 1983.

Michell, John, *The Little History of Astro-Archaeology*, Thames & Hudson, London, 2001.

Newall, R.S., *Stonehenge*, HMSO, London, 1975.

Newham, C.A., *The Astronomical Significance of Stonehenge*, Moon Publications, Wales, 1972.

Nuegebauer, O., *The Exact Sciences in Antiquity*, Dover, New York, 1969.

Pacioli, Luca, *Francesca and da Vinci. Summa di arithmetica, geometrica, proportione et proportionalita*, Venice, 1494.

Pacioli, Luca, *De divina proportione*, 1509. (illustrated by Leonardo da Vinci)

Pacioli, Luca, The Divine Proportion, Abaris Books, Norwalk, 2006.

Pappas, Theoni, T*he Joy of Mathematics*, Wide World Publishing/Tetra, San Carlos, 1989.

Pappas, Theoni, *More Joy of Mathematics*, Wide World Publishing/Tetra, San Carlos, 1991.

Pappas, Theoni, *The Magic of Mathematics*, Wide World Publishing/Tetra, 1999.

Pappas, Theoni, *Fractals, Googols and other Mathematical Tales*, Tetra, San Carlos, 2000.

Pennick, Nigel, *Sacred Geometry*, Capall Bann, Chieveley, 1994.

Plichta, Peter, *God's Secret Formula*, Element Books, Dorset, 1997.

Rawles, Bruce, *Sacred Geometry Design Sourcebook*, Elysian Publishing, Nevada City, 1997.

Richards, Julian, *Stonehenge*, English Heritage, Swindon, 2005.

Rubenstein, Richard, *Aristotle's Children: How Christians, Muslims and Jews Rediscovered Ancient Wisdom and Illuminated the Dark Ages*, Harcourt, New York, 2003.

Schimmel, Annemarie, *The Mystery of Numbers*, Oxford University Press, New York, 1993.

Schneider, Michael, *A Beginner's Guide to Constructing the Universe—The Mathematical Archetypes of Nature, Art and Science*, Harper, New York, 1995.

Skinner, Stephen, *Living Earth Manual of Feng Shui*, RKP, London, 1982.

Skinner, Stephen, *The Magician's Tables*, Golden Hoard, London, 2006.

Sobel, Dava, *Longitude*, Penguin, London, 1996.

Index

Stewart, Ian, *Nature's Numbers*, Weidenfeld & Nicolson, London, 1995.

Stirling, William, *The Canon: An Exposition of the Pagan Mystery Perpetuated in the Cabala*, Elkin Matthews, London, 1897.

Stukeley, Rev. W., *Stonehenge, a Temple Restored to the British Druids*, London, 1740.

Stukeley, Rev. William, *Avebury, a Temple of the British Druids*, London, 1743.

Tennent, R.M., *Science Data Book*, Oliver & Boyd, Essex, 2001.

Thom, Alexander, *Megalithic Sites in Britain*, OUP, Oxford, 1967.

Tokaty, G.A., *A History and Philosophy of Fluid Mechanics*, Dover Publications Inc., New York, 1994.

Vitruvius, *Ten Books of Architecture*, Dover, New York, 1960.

Walser, Hans, *The Golden Section*, The Mathematical Association of America, Washington, 2001.

Walter, Katya, *Tao of Chaos*, Element Books, London, 1996.

Watkins, Alfred, *The Old Straight Track*, Garnstone, London, 1970.

Wilkes, John, *Flowforms The Rhythmic Power of Water*, Floris Books, Edinburgh, 2003.

Wilson, Colin, *The Atlas of Holy Places & Sacred Sites*, Dorling Kindersley, London, 1996.

Page numbers in *italics* indicate illustration captions.

3-D spiral 48
9: 127
10: 18, 21
16: 20
81: 20–1

Adelard of Bath 41
Age of Aquarius 80
Age of Pisces 80
Alberti, Leon Battista 10, 128, 142, 144
ammonite 67
ancient monuments 93
ancient peoples
    astronomy 74, 75
    buildings 13
    measures 25, 26
    sacred spaces 6
angles 44
    trisecting 47
animals 66–7
Apollonius of Perga 43
Arabs 8, 38, 84
Arago, François 83
Archimedes 43, *43*, 56
Archimedian solids 56–7, *57*
Aristotle 9
astro-archaeology 102–5
astrology 77
astronomically aligned structures 77
astronomy 8, 75–81
Athena Parthenos 124, *124*
Aubrey, John 102, *102*, 103
Aubrey Holes 103
Avebury 103–4, *103*
Avenue, Stonehenge 110–11

Babylonians, astronomy 77
Bacon, Roger 141
Baigent, Michael 150
Bauvel, Robert 80
beauty, ideals 41
Behrend, Michael 30
Bell, Johann Adam Schall von *85*
Bergers d'Arcadie, Les (Poussin) 149, 151, *151*
Bernard of Clairvaux, St 134
Bernoulli, Jakob 48
Big Dipper 81, *81*
Billingsley, Sir Henry 41, 93
Bouvelles, Charles *51*
Brahe, Tycho 79
Bramante, Donato 9, 128
Bright, Greg *113*
Brown, Dan 38, 147, 150

Brunelleschi, Filippo 142, *142*
building construction 9
Butler, Alan 31

caduceus wand 72, *72*
Caesariano, Caesar 132, *133*
calendars 84–5
Callanaish stones 7, *105*
Camden, William 94, 102
capstone, pyramid of Ramose *28*
cartography 82–3
Castlerigg Stone Circle *29*
cathedrals, Gothic 9, 116
Centre for Crop Circle Studies 114
Chalice Well, Glastonbury *131*
Chartres Cathedral *11*, 113, 134–5, *135*
Chinese 84
Christianity, symbols 130–1
churches 10, 11
circle 48, *48*
    squaring the 46, *46*
composite numbers 32
composition, paintings 148–9
conchoid 51, *51*
Copernicus, Nicholaus 78
Cornford, Christopher 151
Crick, Francis 72
crop circles 114–15, *115*
crystals 64–5
cube 54, 55, *55*, *57*
    doubling 46–7, *47*
cubic crystals 65
cubit *30*, 31, *31*
cuboctahedron 57
curves 48–51
cycloid 50–1, *51*

da Vinci, Leonardo *see* Leonardo da Vinci
Da Vinci Code, The (Brown) 38, 147, 150
Dee, John 93–5, *95*
    Euclid 41
    mapmakers 82, 146
    megalithic sites 90, 102
    optics 141
    Rudolph II: 79
denominator *see* divisor
deoxyribonucleic acid *see* DNA
Descartes, René 48, 50
Devereux, Paul 99
direction, sacred structures 11
divina proportione, De (Pacioli) 144, 145
Divine Proportion *see* Golden Mean
divisor 24
DNA 72–3, *73*
dodecahedron 54, 55, *57*
dog star 80

Dome of the Rock mosque 123, *123*
double helix 72
double pentagon 73
dragon veins 99
duals, geometric 55
duplicating a cube 46–7, *47*
Dürer, Albrecht 143, *143*

earth, circumference 26–7, *27*
Egyptians
    calendars 85
    pyramids 12, 117–21
    sacred space 91
    surveying 52
elements (classical) 54, 55
Elements (Euclid) 41, 42, 93
elements (periodic table) 21, *21*
ellipse *48*, 50
equi-angular spiral 48, 63
equilateral triangle 45, *45*
Eratosthenes 26, *26*
Euclid 6, 41, *41*, 42, 93
Eudoxus of Cnidus 42
eurhythmy 129
even numbers, *lambda* 18

feng shui 11, 20
fern *63*
Fibonacci series 10, 38–9, *38*, 63
fish symbol 130–1
Flagellation of Christ, The (Piero della Francesca)
    148, *149*
flying buttresses 134, *135*
forms, repeating 9–10
Fortune, Dion 99–100
fractals 58–9, 70
fractions 24–5
France 31, 87
freezing water 71
Fuller, Richard Buckminster 138
Funck-Hellet, Dr 149

Galileo 50, 86, *87*
Gaudí, Antonio 138, *138*
genetics 72–3
geomancy 20
geometric fractals 58
geometry 6
    Arabs 8
    Greeks 7, 15, 40, 41–3
    plant growth 63
    projective 146
    sacred 6–8
    unanchored 91–2, *91*, *92*
Giorgi, Francesco 19
Glastonbury Abbey 92, *94*

Glastonbury tor 12, *99*, 100
Glastonbury Zodiac 94
God, name for 21
Goethe, Johann Wolfgang von 138–9
Golden Angle 63
Golden Mean 8, 34–9, 48, 63, 73
    see also phi
Golden Number *see* Golden Mean
Golden Pentagram 37–8
Golden Ratio *see* Golden Mean
Golden Section *see* Golden Mean
Golden Triangle 36–7, *37*, 45
Gothic cathedrals 9, 116
Great Pyramid 28, 80, 117, 119
Great Pyramid triangle 45
great rhombicosidodecahedron *57*
great rhombicuboctahedron *57*
Greeks
    geometry 15, 40, 41–3
    sacred geometry 7
    temples 12, 91
Greenwich meridian 74, 83, *83*
Grosseteste, Robert 141

halite *64*
Han Ying 71
harmony 6–7, 16, 23
Hawkins, Gerald 102
Haytham, al- 141
heavenly bodies 18
height, pyramids 118–19
heliacal rising *81*
helix 72–3
Herodotus of Halicarnassus 112, 120–1, *120*
Heron of Alexandria 43
Herschel, Sir John 80
hexagon 45
hexagonal crystals 65
hexagram 45
hexahedron 54, *55*, *57*
Hipparchus of Rhodes 43, *43*
Hippasus of Metapontum 36
Hippocrates of Chios 50
Hogarth, William *143*
Hooke, Robert 71
horns 66–7, *67*
Hoyle, Fred 102
Huygens, Christiaan 136
Huysmans, Joris Karl 83
Hypatia of Alexandria 43
hypotenuse 52

Iamblichus of Chalcis 36
IAO 21
ice crystals 71
icosahedron 54, *55*, *57*

icosidodecahedron *57*
Iktinos 126
incommensurate numbers 36
involute curve 50, *50*
irrational numbers 34, 40, 52–3
irregular polygons 54
Islamic world 9
isopsephy 21, 121
Isosceles triangle 45, *45*

Jacopo de'Barbari 144
Jerusalem *122*
Johnstone, Colonel 110

Kelley, Edward 93, 94, 95
Kephren pyramid *119*
Kepler, Johannes 75, *79*
    Archimedean solids 56
    ellipse 50
    planetary orbits 9, 43, 50, 74, 78–9
    snowflakes 71
Kepler's constant 79
Khafre pyramid *119*
kilogram, standard *86*
King's Chamber, pyramids *121*
Knight, Christopher 31

labyrinths 112–13, 134–5, *135*
lambda 16, 18–21, *19*
Lamy, Lucie 92
Last Supper, The (Leonardo da Vinci) 146–7, *147*, 148
latitudes 82
Laue, Max von 64
leaf spacing 63
Leda and the Swan (Leonardo da Vinci) 149, *149*
Leibniz, Gottfried Wilhelm 50
Leonardo da Vinci 128
    architecture 9, 10
    Last Supper, The 146–7, *147*, 148
    Leda and the Swan 149, *149*
    Pacioli 144, *145*
    perspective 146–7
    Vitruvian man 128–9, *129*
Leonardo of Pisa 10, *38*
ley lines 20, 96–101
Lincoln, Henry 83
Lindeman, Ferdinand von 46
lines of sight 98
Livio, Mario 8, 91
Lockyer, Sir Norman 102, 104–5, 107, 110
logarithmic spiral 7, 48–9, 66
London 139
longitudes 82–3
Louis XIV: 83
lune 50, *50*

Magdala Tower, Rennes-le-Château *150*
Maiden Castle *101*
Maltwood, Kathryn 94
Mandelbrot, Benoit 58
Mandelbrot set *59*
manmade world 89
map grid *82*
mapmaking 82–3
mazes 112, *113*
meandering rivers 69, *69*
measurement 25, 26, 28–31, 86–7
megalithic sites 13, 74, 90, 93, 102–5
megalithic yard 30–1, 105
Menaechmus 42–3
Menelaus of Alexandria 43
Mercator, Gerard 82
meridians of longitude 82–3
metonic time period 85
meter 87
    standard bar *86*
metric system 31
Michelangelo 10
Michell, John 96, 100, 102
Milan Cathedral 132–3, *132*, 133
monoclinic crystals 65
moon 76, *76*, 84
mosques 10
Mounteagle's land 95
music 8, 18, 22–3

natural fractals 58
nature 61, 62
nautilus 66, *66*
Newham, C. A. 102
Newton, Sir Isaac 50, 136
Nicomedes 51
ninths 25
noumenal world 15
numbers
    composite 32
    even, *lambda* 18
    incommensurate 36
    irrational 34, 40, 52–3
    odd, *lambda* 18
    prime 32–3
    Pythagoras 16
    round 29
    whole 8–9, 16

octahedron 54, 55, *55*, *57*
odd numbers, *lambda* 18
Old Sarum *101*, 106–9, *109*
Old Sarum-Stonehenge ley 107, *107*, 110
optics 141
organic architecture 138–9

Ortelius, Abraham 82
orthorhombic crystals 65
Osirion 92

Pacioli, Luca 143, 144–5, *144*
painting 142–3
    geometric analysis 148–9
Palazzo Strozzi *35*
palm 31, *31*
Pappus of Alexandria 43
parabola 48, *48*, 50
parallels of latitude 82
Paris meridian 83
Parthenon 13, 92, 124–7, *125*, *126*, *127*
Pascal, Blaise 50
patterns, repeating 9–10
pendulum 87
Penrose, F.C. 104
pentagon 35
    double 73
pentagram 37
perch 105
periodic table of the elements 21, *21*
perspectival lines 148
perspective 142–3, 146–7
perspective machines *143*, 146, *146*
petal numbers 63
phi 16, 34
    Fibonacci series 39
    Great Pyramid 119
    pentagons 73
    plant growth 63
    spiral 48
    see also Golden Mean
pi 46, 119
Piero della Francesca 143, 144, 148, *149*
place names 97
planets 18, 78–9, *78*
plant growth geometry 63
Plato 42, *42*, 54
Platonic solids 54–5, *55*, *57*
Plichta, Peter 21
Pliny 112
Plough 81
Polaris 75, 80
pole 105
Pole Star 75, 80, *81*
polygons 54–5
polyhedron 54
Poussin, Nicolas 149, 151, *151*
power lines 99–100
power spots 11
precession 80
prime meridian 74, 82–3
prime numbers 32–3

Priory of Sion 150
projective geometry 146
proportions 7
Ptolemy, Claudius 43
pyramid 55, *57*
pyramids (Egyptian) 117–21
Pythagoras 9
    numbers 16
    Pythagoras' Theorem 17, *17*, 44
    Pythagorean Triplets 17–18, *18*
    vesica piscis 131
Pythagoras' Theorem 17, *17*, 44
Pythagorean Triplets 17–18, *18*, 52

quadratrix 47
quadrivium 8

random fractals 58
ratios 29
rectangle, root 53
recursive mathematical function 59
regular polygons 54–5
Renaissance 9–10, 19, 140
Rennes-le-Château 150
repdigits 127
repeating patterns 9–10
rhombohedral crystals 65
right-angled triangle 44–5, *44*
rivers, meandering 69, *69*
rod 105
Rogers, Sir Richard 139
Romans, calendars 84
root rectangle 53
round numbers 29
royal cubit 31
Rudolph II: 79
Ryan, Paul 139

sacred feminine 130
sacred geometry 6–8
sacred spaces 10–12, 89, 91–2
Sagrada Familia cathedral, Barcelona 138, *138*
Salisbury Cathedral *106*
salps 67
Santa Croce Monastery *145*
Saunière, Berenger 150
scales (music) 22–3
Schauberger, Victor 68
seasons 76
seedheads 63
seked 117–18
sextant *82*
Sforza, Ludovico 144
sieve of Eratosthenes 33
sighting points 76–7
Simson, Robert 63

Sirius 80–1
small rhombicosidodecahedron *57*
small rhombicuboctahedron *57*
snowflakes 70–1, *70*
snub 57
snub cube 57
snub dodecahedron *57*
solids
    Archimedian 56–7, *57*
    Platonic 54–5, 55, *57*
Solomon 122
Spence, Kate 80
Sphinx *120*
spiral 48–9, 66–7, *69*
squaring the circle 46, *46*
St. Mary's Cathedral, San Francisco 139, *139*
St. Paul's Cathedral, London *136*, 137, *137*
St. Sulpice, Paris 83, *83*
standard cubit 31
standards, units 86–7
standing stones 11
stars 75, 77, 80–1
Steiner, Rudolf 138–9
stone circles 102
Stonehenge 97, 102, *102*, 103, 110–11, *111*
Stonehenge-Grovely Castle ley 110
Stonehenge-Old Sarum ley 107, *107*, 110
structures, astronomically aligned 77
Stukeley, William 102, *103*, 104
Sully, Henry 83
sun 75–6, *76*
sunflowers 63
surveying 52
Sydney Opera House *13*, 139, *139*
Syon House, London 93

Talleyrand, Charles de 87
T'ang Chin 71
tau 34
Temple of Solomon 12, 122–3
temples 10, 11
Ten Books of Architecture (Vitruvius) 128
terminals, ley lines 107–8
tetractys 18, *18*
tetragonal crystals 65
tetrahedron 54, 55, *55*, 57
Thales of Miletus 42
Theaetetus of Athens 42
theodolites *27*
Theon of Alexandria 41
Thom, Alexander 102, 105
time, measuring *25*, 84–5
treasure sites (Dee and Kelley) 94–5, *94*
triangle 44–5
    surveying 52
triangulation 52, 100

triclinic crystals 65
trigonal crystals 65
trisecting an angle 47
trivium 8
truncated cube 57
truncated dodecahedron 57
truncated icosahedron 57
truncated octahedron 57
truncated tetrahedron 56, 57
truncation 57
Tyler, Major 100

unanchored geometry 91–2, *91, 92*
unicursal labyrinths *112*, 113, *113*
unicursal triquetra *131*
units of measurement 25, 26, 28–31, 86–7
university curriculum, Middle Ages 8

vanishing point 142, 146
vesica piscis 130, *131*
vision 141

Vitruvian man (Leonardo da Vinci) 128–9, *129*
Vitruvius Pollio, Marcus 9, 91, 126, 128, 129

Wailing Wall 123
Wallis, John 136
water 68–9
    freezing 71
Watkins, Alfred 96, 98
Watson, James 72
whole number ratios 22
whole numbers 8–9, 16
Wilkes, John 69
Wilkins, Maurice 72
Wren, Sir Christopher 9, 87, 136, *136*

Yarnbury Castle *108*
Yates, Reverend 20

Zodiac 75

Acknowledgments

Editor
  Camilla Davis
Executive Art Editor
  Leigh Jones
Project Designer
  Patrick Nugent
Illustration
  Laurent Brindeau
  Jen Mexter
Picture Research
  Emma O'Neil
Production
  Simone Nauerth

Picture Acknowledgments

Key: t – top, b – bottom, l – left, r – right
akg-images 19, 143 t & b, 148, /Pietro Baguzzi 147, /Cameraphoto 129, /Erich Lessing 144, 151, /Rabatti-Domingie 140, 149 t, 149 b; **Alamy** /Albaimages/Ronald Weir 90, /Atmosphere Picture Library/Bob Croxford 94 t, 131, /Bildarchiv Monheim GmbH/Florian Monheim 106, /Peter Bowater 69 t, /Bruce Coleman Inc/Edward R. Degginger 64, /CuboImages srl/Nico Tondini 145 b, /Ian Evans 59 r, /eye35.com 29, /Michael Foyle 11 r, /Hidoe Kurihara 132, /Eddie Linssen 12 b, /Malcolm MacGregor 105, /Niall McOnegal 83 t, /Mary Evans Picture Library 87, 150, /Phototake Inc/Image Shop 72 t, /Rough Guides 139 t, /Skyscan.co.uk 101 b, 99, /travelshots.com 138, /WorldFoto 13 b, 139 b; **The Art Archive** The British Museum/Eileen Tweedy 2, /Egyptian Museum, Turin/Dagli Orti 28 r; **Bayerische Staatsbibliothek München** Clm 14731, fol. 82v 112; **Bridgeman Art Library** /Acropolis, Athens, Greece 125, /Bibliothèque de la Faculté de Medecine, Paris, France, Archives Charmet 16, 20, /Bibliothèque des Arts Décoratifs, Paris, France, Archives Charmet 23 t, /Bibliothèque Inguimbertine, Carpentras, France, Giraudon 14, /Bibliothèque Nationale, Paris, France, Giraudon 9, 145 t, 133, /Bibliothèque Nationale, Paris, France, Lauros/Giraudon 26 t, /Museo Archeologico Nazionale, Naples, Italy 120 t, /Private Collection 146, /Private Collection, The Stapleton Collection 26 b, 93 b, 104, /Stapleton Collection, UK 121, 122; **Christie's Images** 41 b; **Corbis UK Ltd**/Jason Hawkes 101 t; **Digital Vision 7; Arwyn Dreamwalker 40; Fortean Picture Library** 115 t & b; **Getty Images** /Jason Hawkes 113, /Photographer's Choice/Stephen Marks 1, 39, 66, /Michael Townsend 13 t, 127; **Iris Water Design & Design, Castleton/www.water-feature.co.uk** 68; **Leigh Jones** 58; **lastrefuge.co.uk** /Dai Sasitorn108; NASA /Akira Fujii 81 br, /Jeff Schmaltz, MODIS Rapid Response Team, NASA/GSFC 60, /Provided by the SeaWIFS Project, **NASA**/Goddard Space Flight Center, and ORBIMAGE 59 l; **National Physical Laboratory** /(c) Crown Copyright 1999. Reproduced with permission of the Controller of HMSO and the Queen's Printer for Scotland 86; **Octopus Publishing Group Limited** 12 t, 62, 69 b, 70 t, 72 b; **Photo12.com** 41 t, 43 b, /ARJ 30, /Bertelsmann Lexikon Verlag 42 t, 43 t, /Oasis 128, 75 t, /Oronoz 124, 136 t, /Ann Ronan Picture Library 93 t; **Photodisc** 50, 66 top left, 74, 76, 88, 97, 116, 119, 120 b, 123, 136 b; **Photolibrary Group** /Mark Hamblin 63, /Index Stock Imagery/Walter Biblikow 83 b; **Illustration based on original drawing by PWS** 91; **Science Photo Library** 38 t, 142, /Dr Jeremy Burgess 11 l, 34, /Scott Camazine 70 b, /Gusto Productions 38 b, /Dale O'Dell 81 bl, /Detlev van Ravenswaay 77, /Sheila Terry 84, /Dirk Wiersma 66 tr, /Frank Zullo 81 t; **Jeff Saward/www.labyrinthos.net** 135 b; **Skinner Inc.** 25, 27 t, 82; Stephen Skinner 19 t, 42, 92, 94 b; **Alison Stones** 135 t; **SuperStock** /age fotostock 67 b; **TopFoto** /The British Library/HIP 30, /The British Library/HIP/Émile Prisse D'Avennes 28 l, /Fotomas 85, /HIP 22 /Charles Walker 94 br, 96.